In Their Shoes

IN THEIR SHOES

Grace Halsell

Texas Christian University Press
Fort Worth

Library of Congress Cataloging-in-Publication Data

Halsell, Grace.
    In their shoes / by Grace Halsell
       p. cm.
    ISBN 0-87565-161-5 (cloth). —ISBN 0-87565-170-4 (pap).
    1. Halsell, Grace. 2. Women journalists—United States—
Biography. I. Title.
PN4874.H2216A3 1996
070'.92—dc20
[B]
                                    96–12868
                                         CIP

The photographs on pages 179 through 194 are from the author's
collection.

Cover and text designed by Barbara Whitehead

Contents

Dedicated to
Ruth Shanks Halsell and Harry H. Halsell
for their valor, love and laughter

Prologue

"Afoot and light-hearted I take to the open road,
Healthy, free, the world before me,
The long brown path before me leading wherever I choose.

Henceforth I ask not good-fortune, I am myself good fortune.
. . . I need nothing . . .
Strong and content I travel the open road."

Song of the Open Road — *Walt Whitman*

*I*n the mid-1990s, the actor Peter O'Toole, promoting his autobiography, told a reporter: "I have been on a journey, without a compass."

A man typically sails off, into the unknown. Yet, in the 1940s, when I embarked on my journey I carried the burden of the known: it was known that woman has always been man's dependent. It was known a woman will find it easier to submit to convenience than work for liberation.

Living as a black maid in Mississippi and working in Los Angeles as "Bessie Yellowhair," a Navajo Indian, I quickly discovered the truth that Goethe spoke: we tend to become what the majority judge us to be. Women of my generation were programmed to become enslaved, to resign ourselves to our lot without attempting to take any action.

I chose, in Whitman's phrase, "to take to the open road."

In addition to an early support system, with some built-in role models close at home — I admired my mother, my older sisters — I list as the second most important ingredient of my life: the place where I was born. The high plains of West Texas had space — and stars I could see at night. My father on warm nights said, "Let's sleep outdoors." We children made pallets and far into the night he talked of his adventures, as my eyes looked to the firmaments, all that was eternity. Later on, I took this sense of space, of openness, with me.

I learned to reject what the world at large might seek, the known, established way. On my journey, to be me, someone I might like to live with, I kept making discoveries of what I did not want in life: I did not want an accumulation of money as my main priority, nor did I want to settle for convenience or comfort. Rather I sought the liberty of experience, and taking that liberty I could roam "the open road" to faraway places and know within myself other continents. Not wanting a frozen face or a set identity for all time, I gave myself the freedom to wear many masks. I sought to be open to life, open to men and women of all colors, creeds and on all economic and social levels. Like Whitman, I am many persons in one. I feel that I am part black, part Bessie Yellowhair, part Mexican wetback; to put it in Whitman's grand phrase, "I contain multitudes."

No one knows the recipe for happiness or truth. In attempting to fashion my truth, my goal was never to strive for "happiness" as such; rather I was aiming for another goal, attempting to gain possession of myself. I have lived a life with greater freedom — and I am convinced with more fun, more laughter, more adventures — than countless men, and I envy no woman, no man. I have lived, for much of my life, with open arms and few if any regrets.

If I had to do it all over again, I'd take a ticket and go! Mistakes and all, all the tears, all the laughter, striking against those known factors as regards women, carrying a suitcase packed with faith and casting myself willingly into the hands of fate, finding it as good a provider as any.

PART

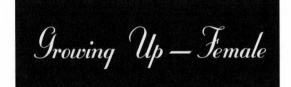

Growing Up — Female

ONE

1: The Beauty of Space

"The only form of thing that we directly encounter, the only
experience that we concretely have, is our own personal life."
—William James

"We live only to the extent that we face up to the world with
all our faculties and as directly as possible."
—René Dubos

Some people travel to the area the early Spanish
explorers called the llano estacado or high staked plains of
West Texas and say they see nothing out there, yet I always
found mystery and beauty in space. Being born in a place
where there was little except space had advantages. Who, I
might ask, am I, amidst this infinite expanse? Not dis-
tracted by skyscrapers, television or a city's teeming
masses, I early on felt a reciprocity with natural forces,
especially wind.

It was a moody companion, often vindictive, uprooting
houses and trees. Then lonely, soul-searching, with shrill,
plaintive moans, crying itself to sleep, leaving the ground
swept clean. Unseen, it demonstrated that what is most
real is most hidden, inaccessible.

I am a product of that open expanse, a flat barren land
with vistas wandering off like a child's imagination. And
born a part of me came a built-in locomotive itch, a fugitive impulse, a driving urge to move across the plains.

Age five, I inserted the steel bit of a bridle into the
mouth of a small horse, a mare I called "Tony." Not own-
ing a saddle, I leaped onto her bareback and, giving free
rein, raced over the bald endless expanse, feeling the har-

mony of my body blending with the onrushing mare. From the time memory serves, I experienced this joy of motion, feeling lifted above the earth, suspended yet sustained by the wind.

I would ride to areas where there was no sound other than the occasional buzz of an insect or the burrowing of a prairie dog. I saw no birds, no plants, no trees. Only the parched plains and the tumbleweeds. Once, at dusk, looking toward the darkening sky and observing the appearance of first one, then myriads of stars, I slid from the small horse, and standing, holding her head, I silently asked: what is the meaning of all that at one moment seems empty, then appears vast, never to end?

It did not often snow in West Texas. And when it did, I studied newly planted pyramids and stars on our window panes, each pattern fragile and unique. I lived in a world of fantasy, and fantasy, said Einstein, means more than any talent for absorbing positive knowledge.

We had few books, no radio or television, little or no cultural events — no opera, ballet, symphony orchestra or even a museum. Yet I was embarked on that greatest of all adventures: viewing the universe, participating in its rituals. I would dig a hole, drop a seed and in time behold a miracle: rambling vines and strange, crinkled, round-lobed leaves reaching out; later I saw the first fruit.

I lay on a pallet at night, overwhelmed by space, attempting to count the stars. I watched a caterpillar transform itself into a butterfly. Might I, also, experience such a metamorphosis, actually change my skin? On another day, I saw a mare's belly shrink and watched a strange bundle drop from her backside and a wet, improbable creature on thin, wobbly legs instinctively hobble to his mother's tits and suckle there.

I saw a bull impregnate a cow. And saw that it was the male on top of the female. The sight was thrust upon me with the force of a sudden flash of lightning or a clap of thunder. I attempted to avert my eyes, as the animals in copulation left me feeling guilty as if party to a crime. In my childhood, I was learning about a subject that was taboo, not discussed by parent to child or in open society.

Once a cow was having trouble giving birth, and my father went to assist her. He returned with his clothes bloody with the afterbirth. No one discussed "life," how it began or how it might end or if one might find or give meaning to the awesome mystery. In the year of 1928, I wore dresses Mother made from bleached Blue Bonnet flour sacks with bloomers reaching to my knees. My hair-style was short, in a bowl style, with bangs. I was chubby, pigeon-toed, tomboyish. I had no playmates who were girls but rather was fully engaged in attempting to enter the circle and be accepted by my older brothers — Oscar Ed, seven, and Harry, nine. I was guinea pig for their games, such as one which consisted of one brother taking one of my hands as in a vise and squeezing until I said "calf-rope," a code word they invented meaning stop. Pretending to be brave, I would suffer, refusing to say their code words, preferring to endure the pain.

With my brothers, I learned to endure. With Louis, my playmate, I made a new discovery: I could lead. Because of the insights he gave me about myself he has remained in memory as I first knew him.

Newly arrived in the neighborhood, Louis, no doubt lonely for companions, walked the short distance from his large, newly-constructed two-story brick home. My brothers and I were scrubby, in rough attire. Louis, five, looked like Little Lord Fauntleroy, dressed in knickerbockers, jacket and laced-up shoes. Entering into our circle, Louis, eyeing me, also five, announced boastfully:

"I can fight better than you."

What was this, some sort of primordial instinct, to prove himself the master of another, the stronger one who would lead? He raised his mitts and I mine, my brothers gleefully urging us on. Oscar Ed, having previously christened me "Goot," now called Louis by a name to rhyme, shouting to him:

"Hoot! Get in there! Hit her, Hoot!"

Louis was lighter on his feet, but I landed heavier blows forcing Louis to bow from the fray. In retrospect, proving myself, as a female defeating a male, was instructive. I was not a breakable commodity, a doll-creature to be dressed in frilly clothes and protected. It felt good to have accepted a challenge, to have fought and wrestled in the dirt. And having gained a victory, I knew greater self-esteem.

Until I met Louis, I was on the outside looking into the world of males, my brothers and their friends. They owned .410 and BB guns and depending on their whims allowed or disallowed my tagging behind them as they hunted rabbits and mourning doves. In their eyes I was a lesser being, younger and worse, mere female. After our first encounter, however, I felt master over Louis.

Each morning, awakening, I quickly dressed and ran to his home where black Sarah — Sa-Sa, Louis called her — patiently dressed him, bending to lace his shoes. Then Louis and I climbed onto the bareback of Tony and explored the plains.

"Goot," he said, as he sat behind me, "let me lead awhile." He wanted to be up front, to hold the reins. "Oh no," I said. "I know more about horses."

Louis asked his mother for his own pony. And soon he had King. But when Louis tried to bridle King, the little horse clenched his teeth.

"Goot," Louis said, "make King open his mouth."

I placed a hand alongside his teeth, moving far to the back of his jawbone, and working from there, forced open his mouth, inserting the bit. A simple story, yet how significant for me the role that Louis played in my early life, allowing me to see a more positive picture of my worth than my brothers supplied.

Memories now seem rich, but in my own family home our possessions were few. We had no rugs on the floor. We rented a room to a boarder to get a few dollars. We ate meat only on Sundays and, for some time, we did not own a car or radio. Refrigerators and televisions had not come along. My brothers and I had two sets of clothes: those we wore to church, which after services we replaced with our school-and-play attire. At Christmas, we got new shoes, wrapped in a box and placed under a tree, along with hard candies, walnuts, pecans, apples and oranges. For the first years of my life, I saw oranges only at Christmas. As for toys, we devised our own: kites from newspapers and small sticks; sleds, made from orange crates, which we rode when it snowed, and stilts by which we elevated ourselves to ten feet tall.

Walking on stilts, I knew life as an adventure, a thrill, one that I could create myself.

2: A Horse Knows When You Are Afraid

"A boyish upbringing...is the kind of education a father prefers to give his daughter; and women brought up under male guidance very largely escape the defects of femininity."
—*Simone de Beauvoir*

*M*y father, Harry H. Halsell, who was sixty-three when I was born, bequeathed me three legacies: the idea of willpower and courage, a motivation to travel and become a full human being who incidentally was female and, perhaps most important, the gift of time. In a sense, he created me by his awareness, his tenderness toward me, giving me an assurance that I could go out into the world as Henry James' Daisy Miller, fully prepared not only to accept but to want men in my life.

"Didn't your father ever warn you not to speak to strangers?" asked Tom Curran, head of Europe's UPI bureau back in the fifties when on a Paris-Madrid flight I took the initiative of getting acquainted. "No," I responded. "My father never knew they existed."

My earliest memories are those of my father reaching out to me, taking me into his lap, reading to me and relating stories of how he escaped from Indians. I pictured the scenes he related: when he was five, Comanches riding bareback on paint ponies careened down a hill crying death to the white settlers. I listened to his recollections of the Civil War. "I was five," he told me, "when I saw my father and grandfather returning home, bedraggled, in tattered uniforms." But the stories of Lincoln and the Civil War meant little to me. I was more interested in Comanches.

"Daddy," I would say, "speak Indian to me." And he complied with a gibberish I now imagine to have been a mixture of Comanche, Spanish, and words he created.

One day, armed with Mother's cosmetics, I climbed into his lap. "Daddy, let me paint your face like the Indians."

"All right, daughter," and he closed his eyes and sat patiently. I rouged his cheeks, ran lipstick across his forehead. Then I plaited his long white hair. Eventually I placed a mirror before his face, and, after deliberate study: "Daughter," he said, "you *done* good." He accented the verb in a western way of talking widely used in pioneer days.

He asked me to cut his hair. I worked meticulously. Again producing a mirror, I reaped his accolades: "Daughter, that's a fine job." If I continued such good work, he said, "you can be the best barber in the whole state of Texas!"

As I worked on his hair, he told me stories of his youth: when he was on trail drives with his father, only seven and carrying his own six-shooter, and how he had made his own way in the world since age fourteen with only the equivalent of three years schooling, and how, by age twenty, he had ridden horseback, alone, to the territory — not yet a state — of New Mexico and outfoxed the famed Apache chief Geronimo.

The year was 1880. The railway company putting down tracks to the West gave young Halsell a job guarding cattle at night, protecting them against thieves, runaway stampedes and Indian attacks. One eerie midnight on a lonely desert he drove his herd of two hundred horses and mules into a low basin, surrounded by soapweed with fuzzy tops that shone like men's heads in the dull sheen of moonlight. Halsell, looking toward an open gap, saw a long line of shadowy figures, later determined to be Geronimo and his band. Quickly deciding on a daredevil tactic, he dug his spurs into his horse and, "whooping and hollering like an army of men," darted toward Geronimo's band, and, by this surprise attack, routed the Indians.

After saving several thousand dollars, he again rode eight hundred miles on his horse, Pythias, back to Texas. There were no highways or known paths. "I had one map — the stars," he said. He killed game for food and at night slept under a heavenly canopy.

His stories always had a bottom line: courage can be a shield, fortitude builds character, hardships are blessings in disguise.

His stories also endlessly drove home one theme: you can struggle and become what you were meant to be. Or, as he always put it, "Fight a good fight. Any old log can float downstream." I heard his litanies so often I began to believe that I could go anywhere, knock, ask, seek, and doors would open. I was never told not to climb trees, roll down haystacks or engage in fisticuffs. I never heard, "be careful." In fact, he never seemed to concern himself about our safety. Once a goat chased my brother Oscar Ed, butting him in the behind while our father sat on a fence laughing. On another occasion Oscar almost killed himself tumbling from a tall tree. Another time I sank and almost drowned in a cesspool. We were simply told, "A few hard knocks are good for you."

When he gave us a task to do, he somehow made it into a game. Once he seated my brothers and me before tin tubs filled with fresh corn on the cob. "I'll give any of you a dollar"—a huge amount of money, it seemed to us— "for every ear of corn you find that has an uneven number of rows on it." We shucked all the corn before we learned that every ear has an even number of rows: twelve, fourteen, maybe sixteen, but never thirteen or fifteen.

Always, life was out there to be lived: "Daddy, let's build a big fire," or "Daddy, let's sleep outdoors, under the stars." As we looked heavenward, he related how he grew up "on a raw frontier" and how he began to read widely, becoming self-educated. He quoted to us from Socrates and Aristotle, Shakespeare, Cervantes, Goethe. He quoted long sections of Milton and talked of Pericles, Plato and Homer as if they were next-door neighbors. "We are all sojourners," he said. As for me, there was no reason that I should not start on my journey. "Travel, daughter," he urged. "Get the benefit."

As I look back, I doubt my father had more than fifty dollars when he urged me to travel, to see the world. Yet, as he knew, an idea firmly planted in the mind represents the first step of a journey, motivation being more important than cash in hand. How his words would ring in my mind: "Travel, daughter. Get the benefit." It became a part of my agenda. I wanted to "get the benefit" long before I knew the meaning of the word.

At mealtime, my father, who never dealt with the mundane, took us on flights of fantasy. "Daughter, did you ever see the Panama Canal?" In those days, we were in the depth of the Depression, my father was too old to get any regular kind of job, and we often had only rice to eat. Yet, he clearly was not thinking of the problems at hand nor worrying about them. "Daughter," he once asked, to get my attention, "were you ever on a great ocean liner?" I studied his white hair and sparkling blue eyes. Too baffled to reply, I wondered: what is he talking about? He knew I couldn't have been on a great ocean liner. Yet, even without replying, I was indeed in mind and spirit transported to another world, with the sea around me and I looking out on a vastness of rolling waves. He taught me to live within my imagination as well as in that realm we term reality.

It was my father who taught me how to swim, who took me to my first football game. When I was twelve, he bought an ancient Dodge for two hundred dollars and taught me how to drive. I became his chauffeur. His assumption always was that I would be proficient.

Coming in from junior high, I often found my father sitting at a card table in the backyard under an apricot tree, surrounded by birds, writing his memoirs in longhand. In his late seventies, he yearned for others to share his exhilarating experiences that spanned the time from Abraham Lincoln to Harry Truman.

I was thirteen when he published his first book, *Cowboys and Cattleland*. Saying I'd learn more traveling with him than in a classroom, he took me out of school to drive for him. We traveled around Texas, and he sold copies of his book to libraries and individuals. Often I was embarrassed, watching him set up a card table on a downtown street, displaying copies of his book and hawking them for a dollar a copy. By the 1980s, they had become collectors' items, selling for a hundred and fifty dollars a copy.

When he died in Fort Worth, Texas, on February 4, 1957, *The New York Times* headlined his obituary:

Harry H. Halsell, 96, Indian Fighter,
Texas Rancher who Once Outfoxed Geronimo Dies—
Was Author of Nine Books.

The *Times* story stated facts about his life that seem incredible to those of us living with the amenities of modern life. After working in the territory that later became New Mexico, he rode horseback north to stake out land on the Cimarron River in Indian territory. This was twenty-six years before the formation of the state of Oklahoma.

"A cowboy could simply stake out or claim land by being there and calling it his own," he told me. "Free grass and cheap cattle made it easy to get rich." In 1888, he had a money belt filled with gold, and he returned to Texas.

When he was twenty-eight, he married Julia, thirteen years his senior and the widow of his uncle, Glenn Halsell. My father and Julia were married for twenty years. He managed large ranches in Clay and Wise counties and lived the life of a wealthy rancher and banker. He was being touted for governor.

Then he saw my mother. He left his vast fortune, which by this time would be valued in the tens of millions, to Julia and her children by her first marriage. Marrying my mother when he was forty-eight, he lived another forty-eight years, many of them as difficult as his early days on the frontier.

Yet, I never heard him suggest in any way that he regretted giving up his wealth. Rich or poor, he remained the optimist, always able to make a joke. Fortified by a sturdy personal faith, he rarely found coincidence in any event but rather viewed the remarkable circumstances of his life as part of a divine plan.

Increasingly, we seem to learn all about what we do but not who we are. If we must forfeit a name on the door or a name identification on a desk, we wonder: who am I? My father thought studying one's self was a first priority. Like Montaigne, he believed, "The greatest thing in the world is to know how to belong to ourselves." He could foresee changes and believed that our major educational problem of the future would be teaching people how to use leisure. For many, time is consumed by work—going and returning from work, being on the job and then resting for the next day's work. When do they have time to think? And if the uneducated move into a lifestyle of complete leisure, will they know what to do with their lives? Even the educated have problems: as we have all seen, many workaholics die almost immediately after they lose a job or retire.

In the case of my father, he never had a nine-to-five job. In his seventies, eighties and nineties, he read and wrote, worked in his garden and sold his books. When I was a small child, he relished playing games such as Monopoly, Rook and checkers with me and my brothers. And most of all, he delighted in good conversation, especially if it led to laughter. He knew how to use time, how to enjoy leisure.

He rejoiced in life, accepting each day as a bonus, one to be savored and used in helping others. Countless women and men have told me, "Your father helped me. I was dejected. He inspired me to live a better, happier life." I knew him only when he was poor and old, yet he was ever alert to praise his God and beyond that to make a joke, to see the absurdity, all that is wonderful and ridiculous and humorous about life. Like Rabelais, he knew "it is the prerogative of man/To laugh at life's short span."

"Count no man happy," Sophocles reminds us, "till he dies." Not until Harry Halsell died, not until his life could be judged as a completed tapestry, safe from its turbulence and hardships, did Mother and I and my five brothers and sisters understand fully what a happy man he was. "Oh, I'll always remember," exclaimed Mother, "his coming to the door laughing."

He loomed important to me because he gave me the dream that I could fashion my own life, that I need not be an appendage to any man. My brothers were wont to put me down, to assume they were superior. Yet my father never made that assumption. "Daughter," he assured me, "you can become the person you want to be." He instilled the idea that even as a pre-school child I could "grab hold" of courage, that it was a defense, a protective shield.

I determined to act out a "willed" type of courage, to test my father's philosophy.

The year was 1929. At age six, I sat alongside Louis, also six, on a corral fence, watching a wild, untamed— what we termed an "unbroke"—stallion named Holbrook pacing, snorting fiercely, seeming to blow fire from his large nostrils. Louis threw a challenge: "Bet you can't ride Holbrook."

"Oh," I boasted, "I'm not afraid."

As the stallion pranced near us, I leapt from the wooden fence, grabbed his dark mane and slid onto the stallion's bare back. Together we raced around the corral, and after two rounds, I lunged for a railing and vaulted back to safety.

At supper, my brother Oscar Ed told our father, "Goot rode Holbrook, the wild stallion." Did he want me to suffer a reprimand, to be put in my place? To know that tempting peril was not for females? His statement made little or no impression on our father, who merely noted that I was not thrown because I had not shown fear. "Cowardice," he said, "gives an odor." And he added, quite matter of factly, "A horse knows when you are afraid."

3 : My Mother – Unafraid of Men

"Woman must come of age by herself —
she must find her true center alone."
—Anne Morrow Lindbergh

My father held me in the palm of his hand, but he never closed that hand. My mother, as is perhaps typical of any mother, loved me with a kind of possessive love. Yet, she and I grew in understanding, one for the other. In every important decision I made, she became supportive of me. In time, I saw her as my best friend.

The former Ruth Shanks was born in 1892, in Amarillo, Texas. Her father, Fred Shanks, was a miller, credited with having created the well-known Gold Medal flour. He moved his family to six different towns within ten years, and Mother, one of six children, only two born in the same town, told me, "I guess Papa kept moving us in order to get a better job." But I have wondered if it were not due, perhaps, to a restless nature.

My mother was two months this side of sixteen in 1908 when she married my father. "Mother," I once said, "you were so young! And you married a man older than your father! Didn't your parents object?"

"Yes, I'm sure they did," she told me. "But Dulce" — a Spanish word meaning Sweet or perhaps Sweetheart, which my father had taught my mother — "told them, 'You can object to this or go along with it but whatever way, I'm going to marry her.'" They agreed to approve. My father arranged the ceremony in Fort Worth, bribing a friend to lie about Mother's age to get a license. Then he went to Burton Peale Department Store and purchased her wedding wardrobe, as well as several gifts including a cross with sapphires, a watch with diamonds strung on a gold chain, a bracelet and unusual garters made with a clasp of gold and inlaid with small diamonds. Her mother and father and a few other relatives were present for the ceremony. Then the couple boarded a train for Corpus Christi. Also accompanying them, at the invitation of my father, were two teenage girls: a sister of my mother, Grace, for whom I am named, and one of his nieces named Maude.

I have tried to imagine the fifteen-year-old Ruth going to bed with a forty-eight-year-old man, and once I asked Mother if she was frightened on her first night. Apprehensive?

"No," she said.

"And was he tender with you?"

"Always."

"And Mother, did you cry?"

"Cry? About what? We were all happy and had good times. And we visited San Antonio and saw the old missions."

I had one other question. Had her sister Grace or Maude been curious? Had they asked, "How was it on your wedding night?"

"No," she said. And I should have known. In her day and age, such matters were not discussed.

Shortly after her marriage, her sister Ida came to visit Mother at her home in Decatur. Ida had two suitors: a young man who wanted to be a banker and a young preacher. "Which should I choose?" Ida asked Mother. "I guess I'll pray over it."

"Better not!" quipped Mother. "He will tell you to take the preacher!"

Ida prayed — and married the preacher, W.L. Barr, who became minister of Methodist churches in El Paso and Sherman, Texas, and Phoenix, Arizona.

As did most women of her era, Mother gave birth to all of her children at home. She had Naomi, Margaret and Hortense and then after a respite gave birth to Harry, Oscar Ed and me. My father, having relinquished most of his fortune, kept failing in his attempts to re-establish himself financially. In Hereford, where he and Mother moved from Decatur, he lost what little he had in a cattle venture. He was down to only small change in his pocket.

My father put Mother — now pregnant with me — and Oscar, two, on a train, and he climbed aboard a mule-drawn wagon with the other four children. In that sad state they migrated to Lubbock. Once there, my father took a job in a nearby town called Baileyboro dismantling burned buildings. For payment he received some of the burnt lumber, and with this he built "the brown house," so called because of the dark, burnt lumber. It was in this house I was born in 1923.

"Mother," I once asked, "the family was so poor — were you sorry when you got pregnant with me?"

"Yes," she said, "at the time I did regret being pregnant again." She had five children and deemed that enough. Moreover, she added, "We were never so poor." She admitted she felt embarrassed by her big belly and family poverty and for a while lived in denial of her pregnant state. "Once Dr. Overton came to check on me. And I hid in a closet," Mother told me. "He opened the closet door and said, 'Come on out.' He just laughed at me."

As children, it is often difficult for us to "see" our parents except in the roles they play. In 1969, I became ill in Washington, D.C. I lived alone and was told by doctors to go to a hospital. Instead, I flew to Fort Worth, and since I was too weak to walk, my petite, seventy-eight-year-old mother wheeled me through the airport. I was put to bed in the back room, the room where my father had died, and lying there for some months I began, for the first time, to see Mother as a person. She became a woman with her own distinct characteristics, her special personality. She had lived and shaped her life by accepting the circumstances in which she found herself — a child-bride to a man thirty-two years her senior — and she had been faithful to what in those years most everyone accepted as the woman's role: keeper of the home, bearer and guardian of the children.

In thinking of her characteristics, I think first of her beauty. I have seen photos of Ruth Shanks at the age when my father first saw her, and these remind me of a young Elizabeth Taylor. In the case of the fifteen-year-old Ruth Shanks, she had abundant chestnut hair, a trim, yet well-rounded figure, an exquisitely chiseled nose, and eyes someone described as "bluer than an artist could paint."

Throughout her life, despite her arduous work and countless heartbreaks, she retained her beauty. Even approaching one hundred, she retained a virginal sweetness. When sleeping, her face appeared free of wrinkles and worries. Seeing her face, I thought of a story regarding Michelangelo: he was asked why, in his masterpiece the *Pieta,* would he have Mary holding a thirty-three-year-old Jesus and portray the mother as a sixteen-year-old woman? He said he did so in order to convey her purity. Mother would scoff at the notion her face radiated a purity, as indeed would my sisters and brothers, whose relationships with both Father and Mother were not as smooth as mine. When I asked Mother about that, she said that with the first children "we wanted them to be perfect" and by the time they came to the sixth, "we were more relaxed." I learned late in my life that Mother had become pregnant again after I was born and that she had an abortion, which to my mind required a great deal of courage on her part. I inadvertently learned about the abortion from my elder sisters but they would not give me any detail. "I don't want to discuss that," said Margaret.

In addition to her beauty, Mother was blessed with good health and boundless energy. Growing up, I do not recall her being sick even for one day. I never remember hearing her say she was tired. Yet her chores were endless. As a child, I accompanied her to a Piggly-Wiggly, and I dreaded watching the checkout. She often would not have sufficient money. But the clerk would say, "That's all right. You can pay next time." She usually bought a fifty-pound sack of flour and, after depleting the flour, bleached the sacks, using the cloth for dishtowels as well as an occasional dress for me. She baked her own bread, and on Sundays I watched her wring a chicken's neck — she also taught me how to do it — and pluck its feathers, then cut and fry the chicken for our big meal of the week. In all of my growing-up years, Mother never had the pleasure of going out with the family to eat in a restaurant. She prepared three meals a day year after year, decade after decade.

Unlike modern men and women, who are encouraged to "let it all hang out," the hurts and the pains and the tragedies of your life, Mother kept what was not good hidden from view or conversation and to me she presented only a bright side. She never engaged in gossip or criticized our neighbors. When our neighbor and friend, the mother of my playmate Louis, shot a man, Mother said, "She did a bad thing, but she is not a bad woman." Some of the neighbors turned their backs on Ella. That was a judgmental snobbery Mother never practiced. For her family and friends, she was steadfast, to the depth of her being.

Among the gifts she bequeathed me, I treasure a love of music. Having a piano in the house, in her sense of priorities, was more important than a rug on the floor. She gave room and board to a music teacher in exchange for my lessons in piano. Mother was blessed with a beautiful singing voice, even until an advanced age, and as a child I recall hearing her play and sing "Drink to Me Only with Thine Eyes" as well as "Yours is My Heart Alone."

She allowed me to experience satisfaction in jobs accomplished. Like my father, my mother also knew the uses of praise. "Run," she would say, when I was five, "see if the hens have laid some eggs." Returning with a bounty, I was praised for having found them.

She permitted her children, at any age, to go to the kitchen and be creative. Even as a pre-school child, I learned how to prepare meals, to make beds, to clean house. Since I was not overburdened, I took pride in feeling myself as capable as a grown-up.

Mother demonstrated how resourceful a woman could be even in an era long before the women's movement. She had never worked in an office, but in the depth of the Depression Mother applied for a job in the Works Progress Administration, devised by President Franklin Delano Roosevelt to create work for destitute families. The WPA had opened a sewing room where women were employed to make garments for the needy, and Mother was made manager of this project. I then saw my mother as the breadwinner for the family: it was she who earned the money to buy our food and our shoes.

Another gift she gave me — she taught me that everyone around us was a Very Important Person, which is to say everyone we knew did a job and it was important to us and others. Mother knew the postman — Mr. Bates — by his name. "Run," said Mother on a day when the temperature soared to one hundred degrees and she saw the postman trudging our way. "Get Mr. Bates a drink of water. He might be thirsty." And we knew the iceman. We placed a large card in a window, indicating whether he should leave five, ten or fifteen pounds of ice. Destitute, hungry men often knocked on our back door. Mother never failed to give them food. She seldom if ever said no to a salesman. I stood by her side when a salesman at our door asked her to subscribe to *The Pictorial Review.* We had little to read and Mother knew I yearned for the magazine. "I have no money," she told the salesman, "but how about two chickens?" He readily agreed and I got the magazine.

I think her greatest attribute was a certitude that trust breeds trust. One incident is lodged in memory: it was 1929. My sister, Margaret, was eighteen, and enrolled in a Fort Worth college. Mother set out to drive her there, taking me along. I was six and Mother, thirty-six. We got Margaret to her college, and Mother and I spent the night with distant relatives, one of whom gave me a small puppy called "Preacher." The next day, we were late leaving Fort Worth for the three-hundred-mile return trip to Lubbock. Mother and I were on a lonely stretch of road as dusk turned to darkness. Suddenly our headlights focused on two male figures. She braked. They ran, opened a door, climbed in the back seat. And we were enveloped in silence. I felt strange, uneasy, and clutched Preacher more closely, wondering if he might protect us. Mother regained her normal speed. Eventually one of the men spoke, almost in a whisper:

"Lady, we are hitchhikers, and we appreciate the ride. But you are alone, with a child. You can't trust people, you don't know who we are." He went on to relate that "only today the two of us have been released from a state penitentiary." He admitted they had served time "for robbery and assault."

Except for the car lights, all was darkness. I was enveloped in fear. Then I heard a loud "bang!" like the firing of a gun. It was a blowout of one of our tires. Mother pulled to one side of the road. It was now dark. The young ex-convicts jumped out, repaired the tire, and we eventually rolled into Lubbock.

It was typical of Mother that she trusted the men. And

for her, it was justified. Another incident, regarding her attitude toward men, made an indelible imprint on my mind:

On the day I graduated from junior high, the assistant principal, Mr. Gordon, called me into his office and locked the door. He opened a small box and removed a golden locket and gently placed a chain around my neck, fastening it. Then he declared he was in love with me and wanted to marry me. I recall walking to a window, looking out on the playground. Even then I feared losing my freedom, and perhaps I was thinking I was being thrust into becoming an adult woman when I was not ready.

Turning toward him, "Mr. Gordon," I said. "I am only fifteen years old."

"No, no," he insisted, indicating he thought me mature. "You are much older."

I asked him to unlock the door. Then I ran the two-mile distance to our home and flung myself across a bed, sobbing uncontrollably. Mother came and sat beside me. "Mr. Gordon," I blurted out, "says he loves me." At that, Mother startled me with her surprising response. She simply laughed. Perhaps she was prepared for something more serious.

"Well," she said, "I think Mr. Gordon means well."

I had never gone out on a formal date, but when Mr. Gordon asked me to go for drives at night, my mother let me make the decision. I went with him once or twice, and I recall jamming myself against the door on my side of the car, thinking: "I hope that old man doesn't try to touch me." Then in his mid-thirties, Mr. Gordon to my young eyes appeared quite old. School was out and I eagerly left for a visit with relatives in another town. He learned my address, and he wrote many letters. They were long, I surmised, because the envelopes were fat. I did not want to know the contents. I burned all the letters, unopened.

"You all die at fifteen," commented the eighteenth-century French writer Diderot to a young woman. He suggested that female adolescents give up themselves as individuals when they become involved with the opposite sex. Mother, with her trust in me, in her summation that "Mr. Gordon means well," had in essence said, "Your life is your own. It is your choice."

Without knowing that Diderot phrase, "You all die at fifteen," I sensed it could have happened to me had I not known that a bigger, fuller, more enriching life was out there as long as I had the courage to go and seek, to follow my star. I had only to take the open road.

In her era and place, Mother like millions of other women had no future except through marriage. I once commented that she had married before her three sisters, Grace, Ida and Florence. "Yes," she said, "I escaped." She indicated that for her it would have been a tragedy to have remained a spinster. Since she was more than three decades younger than her husband, her children often acted as her peers. I think of how back in the forties I announced to her, quite without preamble, "Mother, I am going to marry Andy." She was washing dishes, and she took her dishtowel with her to a chair in the living room, where she sat, hoping to dissuade me. "You need not waste your time talking," I bluntly informed her. It was a settled matter. And she cried. Soon she dried her tears. And became supportive, never once voicing any criticism of him, determined to see only good in him and in the marriage.

I came to realize how deeply I loved her when at age ninety-two — still active, still driving her car, shopping and cooking for big family reunions — she fell and broke a hip and for several months was unable to walk or care for herself. My three eldest sisters made a decision to sell the home — without telling me — and place Mother in a nursing home. After hearing of the decision, I flew immediately to Fort Worth and on my knees, crying, said,

"Mother, you don't need to leave your home. I will stay with you."

"No," she said. "You go on back to Washington."

She knew — and I knew — that the elder sisters would break with me and who knows, perhaps with her, if I took charge. And could I effectively do so?

Mother had struggled to mold a family, to keep us together. She was willing to stay in her role, to make a sacrifice, to do what her three older daughters said was best. She was always flexible, using her shrewdness to get around, over or above a problem, but she could bend, when necessary, to forces beyond her control.

I had seen my mother care for my father, in his eighties and nineties, when she was still relatively young. Then in her late years, she was without family, in a nursing home, reportedly "the best," but with a staff of young and uncaring workers. I flew to Texas every few weeks to visit. Always I was struck by the fact that it was filled with old women. We are a society of men and women who look after men. Then when women reach old age, they are too often lonely and alone.

All the hardships and pains I have suffered in my life together would not equal what I felt seeing my mother sitting in a nursing home. She taught me one final lesson: helping her out of there was what I most wanted, and one does not get everything one wishes for in this life.

The blows in life can be swift. The same week that Mother broke her hip, my sister, Naomi, was told she had cancer. And before long she died. And my sister, Hortense, was told she had cancer, and we watched her die. And my brother Oscar's wife Betty was told she had cancer, and she too died.

Mother's mind remained sharp. Of the deaths she said, "It seems like a bad dream."

I believe Mother chose the day she would die, the nineteenth of August, 1992. She had observed her hundredth birthday in May and kept her keen mind to the end. Her hair had never turned gray, she had all her teeth, and her eyesight was sharp. When she was dying, I had a premonition, as one says, a certitude that comes without knowing how. I left Washington at six-thirty in the morning, and Mother died in her sleep while I was en route to her. I was left with another certitude: her love is and has been all my life my greatest ballast.

Decatur, just north of Dallas-Fort Worth, was where my father grew up, where Mother and my father met, and where five of their children were born. There is a beautiful, quiet cemetery there, with oaks and gently rolling hills. Many of the old-timers in the Halsell and Waggoner families, related through various marriages, are buried there. Standing at Mother's gravesite, I felt the warmth of a brilliant sun as well as a refreshing cool breeze. Before Mother was put into the earth, a multitude of gorgeous butterflies arrived, hovering over and around her. In their beauty and delicacy, they, like her, signified a miracle to cherish.

Even years after her death, I know where to find her. When I walk in a nearby park and see beauty I call her name: she is there — in a rose, in the oaks, with the butterflies.

4: Growing Up as "The Baby"

*T*hrough the years I have written often about the influence of my unusual parents but never analyzed the influence of my brothers and sisters. Regardless of my failure to recognize their roles in my life until recent years, my sisters, especially, exerted an enormous influence on me.

In my earliest years, I did not really see them, at least not in the manner that I perceived and interacted with my mother and father, brothers, my playmate Louis, my pony and our dog, Luke. I seemed to catch only fleeting glimpses of my older sisters, who by the time my memory starts to serve were out on a bigger stage of life, going off to college, getting jobs, concerned with their dress, their hair and the men in their lives. I was certain that I belonged in the circle that included my brothers, but those older girls seemed remote, like strangers who came to visit. When I was growing up in Lubbock, I was not the only one who saw them as distant, not fully connected to Harry, Oscar Ed and me.

"Those older girls," asked the grandmother of Louis, when I was five, "are they your real sisters?" Since I did not know, I lived with a doubt not resolved for many years. I eventually came to know that while we six children had the same mother and father, in another sense my older sisters had parents who could be said to be different from mine because the family's economic and social status was drastically changed. My sisters were born in a big ranch home to a mother who by age twenty had three girls. Their father was a virile rancher in his prime. I was born in a more isolated and provincial setting, with a thirty-year-old mother and a father shorn of his wealth, almost seventy and with no paying job or income.

While our father wanted us to exert free will — "any old log can float downstream" — it nevertheless remains true: the most important aspects of our lives are those over which we have no control. These include to whom one is born, who is to be tall, who is the firstborn, as was my sister Naomi, or, like me, the last in line. Needing the help of the older girls, Mother encouraged my sisters to cast themselves in nurturing roles. She did so by telling them to clothe the baby, feed the baby, wash diapers for the baby. My role in a real sense was written for me. I was their "baby," and while I enjoyed the nurturing for many years, when, eventually, I wished to break the baby mold I discovered for my sisters it had been cast in iron.

Early on, however, I benefitted from viewing my older sisters as risk takers and decision makers. My mother in a sense used these sisters to implant in me the idea that they were steeped in talent and self-confidence and imbued with initiative and enterprise and that it would be natural for me also to have these qualities. Since they left home when I was young, I learned their characteristics largely through the stories that Mother told me, stories about when the firstborn was a daredevil, how she, wanting to get her pony in front of a mirror "to let her see herself," rode the little mare up the back steps of the Decatur ranch home and into the bedroom. And another story told of how she coaxed her small horse up the steps of the Wise County Courthouse, then perhaps the most imposing edifice in North Texas. After Naomi started to school, riding her pony and hitching her to a post until classes were dismissed, Mother recalled that in the afternoon, "I would look out a window, and see her racing down a hill at full speed and standing on her pony!" The Decatur ranch house was isolated, the nearest neighbors, the Fillingims, a mile or more, across a creek. Once when Father was out of town two decades before I was born, Mother was alone with her three small girls. "It was a bleak winter night," Mother related, "and I was holding Baby Hortense. She was suffering with membranous croup and at times not breathing, apparently dying." Whereupon Naomi, seven, "didn't hesitate a moment. She got her coat and started out," and here Mother's eyes filled with tears, reliving the episode of that cold night, her brave firstborn running across a dry creek bed in the dark to get help from the Fillingims. I grew up on other stories — how Naomi leapt into Corpus Christi waves to save a drowning Margaret, how she rescued Oscar Ed, who was being trampled by a horse. Hearing such stories, I was instilled with a dream: I too wanted that kind of courage.

Naomi always questioned authority and often diverged from a traditional path. As a teenager, she "ran off" with a married man and crossed a state line. To do so in her era was a crime. Police stormed a Boston apartment where she was living, and while the man went free she was handcuffed and put behind bars. I was only two, and it was late in my life before I came to know the story of how Father had driven in our old family car, sleeping in parks at night, to get his eldest daughter from a jail in Boston.

Naomi was tall, slender, with shoulder-length red hair, as striking in appearance as the movie star Rita Hayworth. She married Marc, a handsome and jolly man, who wrote, produced and sang on a children's radio show in Detroit. It was one of the big events of my youthful life when in 1939, on the occasion of my sixteenth birthday, Naomi and Marc came to visit, driving a large, black Packard convertible. They also owned their own plane and both had pilot's licenses.

Additionally, they both were amateur actors and went to New York regularly to see the latest plays. On their first evening in Lubbock, Naomi showed photos from a Schenectady, New York, Mohawk Drama Festival. She conveyed the thrill she had known in participating in that festival's staging of Wilder's *Our Town*, directed by Charles Coburn. Naomi — "she's got the most brains of any of my children," said our father — could quote from the Greek playwrights and Shakespeare and poets such as Edna St. Vincent Millay. As she talked about artists and writers, she made them more accessible to me.

Naomi was drawn to the beauty of the Southwest, to Santa Fe and Taos, just as in the early days of its development Lawrence Durrell, Martha Graham and Georgia O'Keeffe had been. On their 1939 visit to Texas, Naomi and Marc decided to continue on to Santa Fe and invited me to join them. I sat in the back seat — the top was down — and they sped along, singing and drinking whiskey from a flask, which left me pondering why persons I admired could act in a manner my upbringing had taught me was wrong. One of the main reasons Naomi wanted to make the New Mexico trip was to see the home of Mabel Dodge Luhan. While not a great writer or artist herself, Luhan had the means to attract and give financial help to a few who were. I knew Lubbock churchgoers might cluck their tongues over Luhan's lifestyle, but Naomi admired her for her ability to break from tradition and live an iconoclastic life, exemplified by her marriage to a Southwest Indian with whom she could not converse — she could not speak his language, nor was he able to speak English.

Both Naomi and Margaret influenced me by their love of music. Mother started piano lessons for Naomi and thought a violin might be right for Margaret. From a Sears

Roebuck catalogue she ordered a half-size or child's violin. As a result when I was a child, I heard Naomi on the piano and Margaret on the violin playing duets such as "To a Wild Rose" and "Believe Me if All Those Endearing Young Charms." Once, as an adult, sitting in a Hong Kong restaurant, chatting with a British gentleman, I became aware of a violinist and familiar strains erased the present. I was transported over time and distance until again I was a child at home, listening to Margaret play the strains I was hearing halfway around the world — Dvorak's *Humoresque*.

"We never had to make her practice," Mother said of Margaret, casting her into a role model of discipline, self-knowledge, knowing her priorities and sticking to them. At age seven, she took instructions from Brooks Morris, known as the best violin teacher in North Texas. Morris traveled a round-trip distance of sixty miles twice a week to give Margaret lessons in Decatur. When nine, Margaret was sent to relatives in Oklahoma City so that she might study with a Mr. and Mrs. Mraz, touted as outstanding instructors. After graduating from high school, she studied violin at Fort Worth's Texas Woman's College, later Texas Wesleyan University, with Carl Venth, a well-known master in the music field who had known Grieg and Wieniawski and had been a choir boy in the Cologne Cathedral. Later, Margaret became first violinist in the Fort Worth Symphony.

One day she met Bill, who also played a violin, but not as well as she. She married Bill and soon put aside her violin. Later, to myself, I posed a question: were the effort, the years of study, of dedication, of achievement all in vain? But in all of life there is an ending, while the melodies one played live on in other lives. As a child I often heard Margaret play in First Methodist Church, and I recall her style, a flamboyance in her attire. I still see her, walking onto the podium, wearing — and this for a morning service — a long, form-fitting red velvet gown. She needed no musical score, but, placing her violin on her left shoulder and closing her eyes, she took her audience into a world of Gounod's "Ave Maria."

To hear Mother tell it, my older sisters were worthy role models: Naomi the most courageous, Margaret the most musically talented, Hortense the most studious. As a child in Decatur, Mother related, Hortense made the attic her classroom. "She was only five, and she would go there, climb up on a desk and play teacher." In 1929, when I was six, Hortense, a high school graduate, applied for work at Lubbock's new Montgomery Ward store.

"How old are you?" asked the manager.

"Sixteen."

And did she think she could handle the job?

"I don't think I can," she told him, "I know I can."

She got the job. And continued working, while she put herself through college. Even with her workload, she made all As and earned her B.A. degree in only three years. Montgomery Ward promoted her to a trainer of new employees throughout the western states. The stores were then installing new cash registers, and Hortense trained employees how to use them. Later she was promoted to a personnel manager, with the responsibility of hiring new workers in the western states. I have seen a photo of her standing by her car in the state of Oregon. Snow-covered mountains are the backdrop, and she appears elegant, wearing a fur coat and hat to match. I also thought she looked lonely. In her early twenties, she was blazing a trail of liberation, driving from town to town over mountain roads, checking into hotels, eating meals alone and coping in a world dominated and managed by men.

In 1943, I received a letter from Hortense, who had married a salesman named Ralph and was living in Manhattan. Her husband, Hortense wrote, would be going overseas. Did I want to come live with her a while?

I was then twenty. I had worked on the Lubbock paper and gone to college for two years. I lost no time in making a decision.

When I went to New York, my sister was thirty and at the peak of her career. She held a job of some prestige and high pay. Later, Hortense had an opportunity to work in London. This was during the height of the fighting in Europe, and she lived through the blitz bombing by the Nazis. On her return stateside at thirty-two, she divorced Ralph and married a second time, and as suddenly as Margaret had given up the violin for role of housewife, Hortense forfeited her career. She became a "total woman," one, that is, totally devoted to serving the desires of her husband. Why, I wondered, when she died — as I reflected on her abilities, her intelligence — had she thrown it all away? Had she found some happiness, to which I was not privy?

Naomi too wanted to express her ultimate femininity. In a long marriage to Marc she had not become pregnant, and, saying she wanted a child more than anything else in life, although she was then near forty, she left Marc and with Max conceived a son. Being "persons" in and of themselves had not, apparently, been adequately fulfilling for my sisters.

PART

The Workplace: Entering a Man's World

TWO

5: Accepted at Face Value

"All professionalized enterprises, whether in business, labor, law, medicine or academic organizations, reveal the same scarcity of women at the top."
— *Barbara Miller Solomon, American historian*

"Any honorable work," so ran one of my father's litanies, "is good."

In West Texas, unlike England, France or even the state of Virginia, we did not have families who belonged to a social register. We all needed one another, and thus we were all important. Having lived through the Depression, being poor was not all that unusual. In a sense we were all beginners, all amateurs.

My first job was as a salesman when I was about five. My father filled small pails of tomatoes from his garden, and I was sent to sell them. Knocking on a neighbor's door, I asked, "Do you want to buy some tomatoes?"

"What do you want for them?"

"Five cents," I said.

I also earned money selling "samples" of Jergen's lotion and Colgate toothpaste and Grapenuts cereal that manufacturers sent free if you but asked. I mailed one-cent postal card requests, then sold the samples to neighbors for ten cents each. And I went door-to-door with magazines: "Do you want the *Saturday Evening Post*?"

"How much is it?"

"Five cents," I said.

In junior high, I began work for a give-away newspaper that had no subscribers and consisted almost entirely of ads. I wrote about church services and piano recitals. With ruler, I meticulously measured my copy and turned in my vouchers. I got paid one cent for every published line.

By the time I entered high school, classes were put in shifts, with some students, myself included, being dismissed in the early afternoon. Like many of my classmates, I went from school to a job. I worked in a small downtown dress shop wrapping packages and as a general cleanup person. I earned twenty cents an hour.

Shortly before I graduated from high school, I walked into the offices of our daily newspaper, the *Lubbock Avalanche-Journal,* to get a job. I had a teenager's pride, believing what I had done in school would be impressive to an adult: I had edited the *Cowboy World* in junior high and for two years the high school's *Westerner World.* I had won most of the state's top awards for high school newspaper work: I had written the best column, the best editorial, and the paper was judged the most outstanding of all high-school newspapers in the state of Texas. Thus I felt confident mounting stairs to the second-floor newsroom. I had no appointment and I knew no one there, but soon I was seated before the managing editor, Charlie Guy, short, rotund, with bald head, pox-marked face and heavy horn-rimmed glasses. He looked bemused, asking, "What can I do for you?"

"I want a job."

"How old are you?"

I had turned seventeen.

"Do you type?"

"I'm learning."

In retrospect, I know there must have been hundreds of older journalists who were looking for a job, this being shortly after the Depression. Still, he dealt with me seriously.

"Are you going to college?"

Yes, I said, I planned to do so. I had been granted a scholarship for Northwestern College of Journalism in Illinois, but we had no money for me to travel there, nor to pay for my living away from home. I chose not to mention that but rather to stick to one point: I wanted and needed a job.

"All right, I'll hire you." But, he added, "you must promise never to study journalism in college. That ruins any potential writer. One should learn by experience." He demanded that I agree. After I nodded affirmatively, he added, "I'll teach you what you need to know."

I moved into a largely male enclave: not only then but in all future jobs, I would be hired by a man. I got assignments from men, they supervised my work, and they approved any promotion or salary increase. I was never in my life hired by a woman, although in several instances I worked alongside them.

When I was starting out, if a woman got a job on a newspaper the editor generally assigned her to write society news, and I was no exception. At the time Guy hired me, I recall only one woman working there, veteran society news writer Margaret Turner. In her fifties, she had a serious, even somber demeanor. A woman who never married, she wore a severe hairstyle, plain dresses and lace-up, heavy walking shoes. She never initiated a conversation that did not have a direct and immediate connection to our work. In thinking back on those days, I have wondered why Guy did not permit Margaret Turner to interview and hire me. It seems clear: he, not she, called all the shots, even all the decisions involving society news.

Besides covering weddings and teas and writing obituaries, I wrote a weekly social column, filled with names and trivia, which Guy personally edited, taking, it seemed to me, a fiendish delight in using a short, stubby black pencil to delete phrases, sentences, paragraphs, and to rewrite my copy to the extent I could never recognize it as my own. With a sardonic sneer, he would shout, "Don't you know how to spell!" Or, "These are not the right initials!" Once I mentioned someone from Tulsa, Oklahoma. Guy, a native of that city, shouted, "Don't ever write Tulsa, Oklahoma! Just say Tulsa. Everyone knows there is only one Tulsa in all the world!"

Back at my desk, tediously typing by my self-taught hunt-and-peck method, I often looked up to find Guy mocking my speed. Folding a newspaper, he furiously fanned it over my typewriter: "Watch her go!" he shouted to the male reporters. "She's setting the place afire!"

Although he was tough as whitleather, I later came to realize I was lucky to have a boss who didn't pamper me. There were other advantages. I began working on newspapers when many executives, especially Texans, prided themselves on their intuitiveness, their ability to "size up" a person. Largely self-made men themselves, they felt that how a person walked, how he or she shook hands—a firm handshake was considered a mark of strong character— and how one looked you "square in the eye" were more important than an impressive résumé. Neither Charlie Guy on the Lubbock paper nor James R. Record, managing editor of the *Fort Worth Star-Telegram*, where I started work in 1945, asked to see a résumé. They focused on me as an individual with potential. They felt one's motivation for a particular job was all-important. Knowing this was the case, I stressed to each how much I wanted the job, how I would diligently apply my energies, my mind. Back then countless Americans, especially, I believe, those of us in Texas, held to a faith, a kind of mantra to which we clung fervently: all that was required of one was to work diligently and you'd make it to the top.

The European conflict represents a second reason why I was able to land a job on the Fort Worth paper. With the Second World War heating up, many male reporters went into uniform, and this presented opportunities for women to move into their former slots. Thus, when Charlie Boatner donned a uniform and vacated the police beat, I became the first woman to cover police for the *Star-Telegram*. In moving me to that beat, city editor Phil Edwards explained, "I've no one else to send."

Arriving at the police department, I saw only men. I met desk clerks, uniformed officers, detectives—all men. There was one exception. When I walked back to the jail cells, I saw women behind bars. Feeling pity, tears came to my eyes. "They're just prostitutes," a policeman said. But I wondered: since a woman does not commit her "crime" alone, why is it always her, and never her partner, who is arrested? The mayor or a rich merchant might have been in her arms an hour earlier, but they were never arrested. Rather, the prostitute was the scapegoat.

On the day the war ended, Edwards asked reporter Madeline Crimmons to call St. Joseph's Catholic Church: "Ask if they will ring the bells to signal peace," he said. In writing her story, Crimmons noted a priest's affirmation that he'd "ring the hell" out of them. Victory in that "good war," as it came to be called, was most real to all who lived through it.

Edwards in time upgraded me from covering police to general assignments and later to amusements editor, writing a daily column. At the same time, I continued to do special interviews and special features. In this period, I began to meet Texans who seemed to stride about in seven-league boots. I was impressed with one characteristic: they were all easy to know.

Amon G. Carter, the *Star-Telegram* publisher, was perhaps the most flamboyant of the Texans. Carter created a legendary nation called West Texas, insisting that this region of desert and scrub was God's country. He appointed himself its official gatekeeper and Fort Worth became "Where the West Begins." Carter, often dubbed

Mr. Fort Worth, had a fetish for giving gifts. Each time I, or any other reporter, interviewed a visiting politician, entertainer or business tycoon, Amon Carter would present the visitor with a Stetson, and a photographer always snapped a photo of his doing so. I knew, in writing identifying cutlines, to say the gift was a Shady Oaks hat, named for Carter's Shady Oaks Ranch.

Carter became close to Elliott Roosevelt after President Franklin D. Roosevelt's son moved to Fort Worth to head a chain of small Texas radio stations. Reporters speculated that Carter made good use of his friendship with Elliott to gain access to the White House. Indeed he pursued FDR relentlessly, camping outside the Oval Office so frequently there was a story among reporters that an exasperated FDR told an aide: "That man Carter is always wanting me to do something nice for Fort Worth, and, if possible, to the detriment of Dallas."

I found Carter's close associate Sid Richardson, a bachelor who lived across the street from the newspaper in the Worth Hotel, a study in contrast. One of the richest men in Texas, Richardson had, according to reports, all his assets "tied up in cash." He did not like publicity and generally shunned social affairs. Once a White House social secretary called "Mr. Sid" and said the president was inviting him to dinner—would he like to come?

"I don't know," Richardson drawled. "What are you serving?"

I also came to know C. R. Smith, largely responsible for getting American Airlines off the ground. I often saw Smith at the *Star-Telegram,* and a couple of decades later in Washington, D.C., I renewed our acquaintanceship after President Johnson appointed him secretary of commerce. Once, introducing Smith to a Washington, D.C., American News Women club gathering, I pointed out that at one time Smith knew, by first name, every employee in American Airlines. He was a manager not removed from his employees, a manager who understood their problems. It was such techniques practiced by early entrepreneurs that made the United States number one in the marketplace.

One day Phil Edwards asked me to cover a Texas hotel convention meeting. "There's about three hundred hotel managers in town. Try to get a feature on one of them." Once at the convention site, I heard that Conrad Hilton was inside an auditorium, listening to a speaker. Where, I asked one delegate, was he seated?

"Down front, about third row from the podium."

I proceeded there, ignoring the speaker on the podium. Spotting my prey, I motioned Hilton to follow me. Not knowing who I was or why he was being summoned, Conrad Hilton rose from his seat, dutifully following me from the auditorium. With both of us standing in a hallway, I interviewed him. And I also told him that the first Hilton I ever visited had been in my hometown.

"So you are from Lubbock!" he smiled, adding, "the other day the *Avalanche-Journal* published an editorial about me, saying how nice it was to have a Hilton there." He beamed with pleasure at that accolade.

I gleaned enough information for two stories, the first dealing with the man himself and how he got started in Cisco, Texas. A second story dealt with his hotel managers and Hilton's technique in hiring them.

"A man's motivation is all-important," he told me. "I found a young man in one of our kitchens, peeling potatoes. And I asked him, 'Young man, do you want to get ahead?' " In the Lubbock Hilton he posed the same question to a man running an elevator. "The primary characteristic I look for is a man's willingness to work, his desire to make good. And in each case, if they convinced me they wanted to work hard and learn a new job, I moved them on up."

I returned to the office and wrote my stories. Later that

day Hilton telephoned me at the *Star-Telegram*, saying there was a convention dinner, given for the hotel delegates, at the 400 Club on Jacksboro Highway, a typical roadside eatery with red-checkered tablecloths. And would I go with him? I did not know, I demurred. I would think it over. If he wanted to call me back, I would let him know. Laughing, he said I should not worry about being safe with him. "I will bring a chaperon, Bob Williford," who was then manager of his Chicago hotels.

I discussed with a few co-workers the pros and cons of his invitation, and when Hilton called back, I said I'd go. That evening, when he knocked on the door of my parents' home, he was in high good humor. He did have Williford in tow. Williford, I noted, was more impressed by going out with the hotel magnate than was I. Hilton was a great aficionado of dancing, and that evening while we were dancing to music by a western band he told me he had four cards printed that entitled the bearer of each to be his personal guest in any of his hotels. He said he was giving one to Mrs. Eleanor Roosevelt. And as I recall, one was for James Forrestal, the secretary of the navy. I do not recall the third name he mentioned, but he wanted the final card to go to me. Back at our table, he produced the last of his special "Be My Guest" cards. Taking a fountain pen from a coat pocket, he signed Conrad Hilton on it. Laughing, he said, "We have Williford as witness" and presented me free entreé to any of the Hiltons.

I used the magic card on many occasions throughout the United States and in many foreign countries. I do not, however, think that the other three persons ever did. At least, each time I showed Hilton's personal "Be My Guest" card to a hotel manager, he gave me a startled look. "It's the first time I've seen such a card!" the manager invariably said. No one, however, ever questioned Hilton's signature. A manager always assigned me a large, splendid room, and on one occasion I was given a sumptuous bridal suite.

Looking back, I am impressed that of the four cards he had printed, he gave two to women. I believe in each instance he gave not for what he could or might get in return, but because he was himself and giving the gifts was what he wished to do. In retrospect, Hilton seems the personification of the confidence expressed in the period following the Second World War. It was a period when one man, with his energy, intelligence and, yes, that word in which he so believed, *motivation,* could build a large, profitable company and have fun doing it.

And what had I done, or could I do, to "earn" his generous gift? Nothing, other than be myself. I was a serious, young reporter, and perhaps he had been impressed that doing my work was more important than having a date with a VIP.

We kept in touch through the years. When we did meet on occasions, in New York and Los Angeles, he always seemed young at heart, eager to hear about my travels in remote climes:

"You say you've been in Chihuahua?" he asked on the occasion of our lunching at the Beverly Hills Hilton. "And what were you doing in Chihuahua?"

"Staying at a Hilton," I confessed.

I used the card for two decades, until the chain of hotels moved more into management, rather than ownership of a property. I always saw his gesture of friendship as a means of his saying, "I see you are striving to be a writer. And I believe in you."

PART

Love and Marriage

THREE

6: Unlikely Love: The Heart Has Its Reasons

"The heart has its reasons/That reason cannot know."
— *Blaise Pascal, French philosopher and scientist*

"We fall in love with our other half."
— *Carl Jung, psychologist*

There must be this thing called "love," as millions testify to its ecstasy, other millions to its pain, silliness, transitory nature. When we experience love, it seems more real than the ground under our feet, but after many years we are often left with a question: what was that all about? "I wonder," I said to one friend of late, "why did I fall in love with Andy?"

"That's often the way it is," he replied. "Usually it doesn't make sense."

In memory, I return to the day I first saw him. A summer day. I was dressed in the mode of the forties, wearing a princess-style dress of gingham, high heels and a straw hat with ribbon at the back. It was my first day on the *Star-Telegram* police beat. I walked five blocks to City Hall and skipped down the steps to the police department, housed in the basement, where there was no air-conditioning. Heat waves, heavily laden with the stench of urine, vomit and insecticides, rose to greet me. A detective stood by a water fountain and a man, broken in spirit, approached him: "I'm on dope," he said. "Please...arrest me." It seemed as casual as a businessman walking into a hotel, requesting to be registered for a night's rest.

Andy the detective — why would I decide I wanted him, more than any other man, then and forever? Who was this person who by chance was standing by a water fountain? Can memory serve to bring him back into my life? He had been on the force as many years as I had lived. I saw him, with wide shoulders, little-boy hips and a lithe, natural form. With the thumb of his left hand he held the jacket of a chocolate-colored, pin-striped, double-breasted suit. His shirt was a checkered red, set off with a blue-and-red striped tie. I was attracted to his panache, to his gun, held in holster on one hip, and to his wide-brimmed hat, cocked low over one eye in Dick Tracy style.

The men had a ritual, leaving, one by one, rambling in what appeared slow motion across Seventh Street to Tubby's. First, Chief Morris invited me, then others. We climbed onto high stools facing a counter and drank from large mugs of coffee, priced five cents, with endless refills. Morris was tall, slow-talking, avuncular, but still with an eye for a young woman. Then there was Detective Gravel, with an omnipresent cigar, and Detective Michaelson, who wore red ties and managed a calculating look even with a toothpick in his mouth.

Only after several weeks did Andy invite me for coffee. In time he would be telling me his stories. Certainly in our backgrounds we were different. Growing up, I had known only faith and trust, while Andy had known the broken home of his parents and later a collapse of his own marital life. It was only in the police department that Andy built the firm blocks of his life. From motorcycle patrolman he became a plainclothesman, and then he was promoted to sergeant and later lieutenant of detectives. Only in the dark, dank, foul-smelling maelstrom of drunks, prostitutes, murderers, thieves, Andy's dungeon and his castle-fortress had he experienced a pattern in his search for orderliness. In a real sense, his code of conduct, his established and rigid set of rules represented, if not his real happiness, then his real self.

I learned to see him as a child, ears too big, barefoot, with ragged shirt, knee-length pants and needing more affection than he ever got. I saw him running across town to find the best watermelon patch and steal what he could carry, and I saw him winging over Chinese elms and diving from high branches into the Brazos. I saw a child eager to help strong-armed crewmen erect a circus tent, and later, when he was a daredevil fifteen, I could see him walking on the wings of airplanes. "You earned a dollar for every stunt," he said. And was he not afraid? "It was not as hard," he said, "as it looked from below."

Andy, whose full name was André Fournier — pronounced in Texas as Four-near — talked to me about his father, an immigrant from France, dubbed by his neighbors "the ol' Frenchman." The father sold vegetables from his vast garden and never permitted Andy to speak a word of French. "You in thisa country," he told him. "Now you speaka English." The old Frenchman divorced Andy's mother, and Andy was told to cook his own oatmeal and wash his ragged shirt. The father brought home a new mother, Celestine. One day when he was still a boy, Andy found Celestine ill and ran for his father. When they returned Celestine was gone.

Soon after my arrival on the beat, Chief Morris, often a guest preacher in local churches, sanctimoniously ushered me into his office, shut the door, and, sitting behind his desk, holding a leather Bible in his oversized hands, read to me from the lyrical Song of Songs. Eventually he motioned me from across the desk: "Come sit by my side." When I was seated in a chair next to his, he read of the whiteness of skin like lilies of the valley and the round firmness of a young maid's breasts that were like pomegranates. And as he did so, the chief cupped a hand over one of my breasts, and later he gently rubbed the palm of his hand up one of my legs. Did I view this as a molestation? A wrong? I stayed passive, feeling, at the core, removed from the scene. Morris talked to me also of raids, arrests, convictions, vice cleanups and sermons he had preached. While I was silent, I secretly was pleading, "Talk to me about Andy, tell me what it was like, in the olden days, when you two met. What was he like as a boy? You knew him then."

"...just a kid," the chief began. "Had worked in a motorcycle repair shop and eventually, out of spare parts, put together a machine of his own. And learned to race it, standing up on the handlebars. He started working here as a motorcycle patrolman, lied about his age. He was sixteen ...claimed he was eighteen. He got married, a petite little thing. And they had two children, and one day, at an unexpected hour, Andy rode his motorcycle home and found her in bed with his best friend. He went crazy, started firing his gun, tried to kill the friend and her. They fled, and later I took him to the country and stayed with him in an old farmhouse for a week, watched him constantly and finally he came out of it." Hearing the story, and perhaps it was not the story so much as the sound of the chief's full, sonorous, resonant voice, I felt an overwhelming desire to rectify Andy's pain. As Desdemona loved Othello for the hardships he had suffered, so in those moments I loved Andy for the pain, the trauma he had known. Young, idealistic, I felt pity, one of the easiest of all emotions to mistake for love.

Always brimming with happiness at being at Andy's side, I registered my pleasure with rapt and close-range attention. I was myopic, needing to wear glasses, but when talking one-on-one, as with Andy, did not do so. One morning, seated at Tubby's, Andy averted his attention from my admiring gaze, blew on his large mug of coffee and said in a low voice:

"You really can 'eyeball' a man."

"Oh, am I too close?"

"It's fine with me. But I wouldn't want to see you doing it with another man. He might not know how to take it, might not understand."

"Understand what?"

"That it's just your way. He might think you were interested in him." Already, and probably in spite of himself, Andy was becoming possessive. But he feared risking his emotions, taking a chance with me. Alone and on his own he had taken the two children from his unfaithful wife and reared them, somehow managing to get them both through college. He had accomplished this by being strong, and he must now feel any indication of a desire for me meant a sign of weakness. His strength was in his loneliness. He lived with it and had made a fortress out of it. On a weekend, Andy and I drove to the scrub oak country to practice with a twelve-gauge shotgun.

"Stand steady," he instructed. "Brace yourself." As he tossed empty tin cans into the air, I fired, almost instantly hearing the ping of a shell as it struck its target. Later as I tossed cans and Andy fired, he consistently missed.

"I'm a better shot than you!" I teased, jumping gleefully. "And you a detective!"

In the fall, Andy and I, together with another couple, drove south near the Mexican border where land holdings sprawl as big as Texas brags. At the ranch, Andy and I struck out alone in search of deer. We hiked for hours, not seeing any game, only the short scrub grass beneath us while overhead the morning sun blazed fiercely. In step behind Andy, I felt the awesome aspect of the infinite space surrounding us and with it a surge of loneliness. Coming upon a grassy knoll, I threw my arms around

Andy's waist and pressed my breasts and stomach and legs against his body.

"Andy," I pleaded, "let's lie in the grass, in the shade, out here, in the open!" I longed to get my arms around the earth, and the earth being too large for my arms, I would settle for Andy. But he was taking it easy with me. Perhaps my zest, exuberance and bouncy joy in life frightened him. We walked back to camp, he talking of the heat, a midday sun and our friends who awaited us.

On another day, we went swimming near Galveston in what then was a pristine Gulf of Mexico. We found sandy beaches that stretched as endless as a child's imagination. In the waters, we dived into high waves, then played as children, I standing on his shoulders or he on mine, each taking turns cradling the other as a small babe in arms, all effortless. At a public pool, I watched Andy dive. Then I walked to the high board. Hesitating, I shouted to him below: "Will you be there if I don't come up?" Lowering my head between outstretched arms, I flung myself to the waters, and to Andy.

Saturday nights we went dancing, to the large Lake Worth Casino ballroom, and here Andy led me with his lively steps, his love of fast tempos and tangos. Even on a social date, Andy wore his Colt .45. Yet, for a moment, on a dance floor, he escaped his persona of armed cop. With the tunes of the forties, especially tangos, he looked like George Raft in the role of Valentino, gliding across a polished floor, bending me as easily as a supple willow branch.

Some months after I met Andy I wrote a story on his promotion from lieutenant to captain of detectives. Having determined to include him as part of my life I felt a vicarious satisfaction that this was happening to him. Sparks of happiness were falling on me, the reflection of them a greater joy than any bounty that might have come directly to me. A newspaper photographer entered the room to take his picture. Andy was a master at controlling his emotions, yet for one moment as he looked at me I saw a smile come to his thin lips, and I noted his narrow eyes shone with happiness.

We often ate dinner at a downtown restaurant called the Mexican Inn, where women in brightly embroidered ponchos served us tacos, tamales and refried beans doused in devil-hot jalapeno pepper sauce. Andy nodded toward a pasty white man standing by the cash register. I knew him as the restaurant owner, who never charged Andy for our meals.

"He was a pimp," Andy said, revealing a private dossier he held on the man. "That was thirty years ago. A two-bit gambler. Matched quarters. And fixed horses. Later he managed a gambling hall, back of the Central Hotel. He paid off the vice squad so his place was never raided. All the city councilmen liked to go there, and the mayor too." Andy gave one of his bitter smiles. "Finally he bought this building, and kept girls, prostitutes, mostly Mexican, upstairs." Now Andy's eyes narrowed like laser beams: "But he loved only one." He paused for me to take full note of that. By now I knew Andy would not say to me, "Let me tell you about my philosophy." Rather, he would relate a parable to reveal it. "He never had anything to do with the others." Then, wrapping up the story, Andy related that Carmen got tuberculosis "and he sent her to El Paso, where she doesn't cough so much, and he takes care of all her bills and calls her every Sunday night." Because the cafe owner had loved "only one," I understood that Andy was telling me not about Carmen or her lover so much as he was revealing his own code of conduct. For Andy, fidelity, constancy, trust, monogamy, in or out of wedlock, represented the highest virtue.

For lunch breaks, we frequently got take-out barbecue sandwiches and picnicked in Trinity Park, where one day, both of us sitting on top of a table eating our sandwiches, he outlined more clearly his code: he never went out with a married woman. "The worst thing you can do, break up a home." And he had never been with a prostitute. Before proceeding he eyed me closely, saying he would never "sleep with a virgin."

In Texas, it can turn from hot to cold faster than a child's moods, and whereas one day we had eaten out in the open, under the trees, the next day it snowed, and we were back at the Mexican Inn. I lowered my head almost to my chili bowl, acting the contrite sinner, and recited a short drama. Tears came to my eyes — I pulled out a name, where the act had occurred, and confessed that the man had taken, but that I had not given. It was a short story, and a true one. And most important, one that I knew Andy was waiting to hear.

He reached to take one of my hands. His eyes were misty, and he left a palm of his hand on top of mine. By placing myself in his arena of operation, I had sealed a bond between us.

The decision was made: we knew we would be together and neither of us felt the need to speak of it. Shortly thereafter, he and I heard of an upcoming trip, which I, no longer on the police beat, would cover for the paper. Logistically, the destination was one in which we would arrive by separate means, and we both knew it would become the destination of our dreams — a place in which our bodies, for the first time, would be joined. Thus a trip of no more than a hundred and fifty miles took on an enormous significance for us. In the town of Brownwood we met, as so often we had, in a coffee shop. Now it was different: he whispered the number of a room, and I later found him there. A sparse room, bare floors, narrow stall for shower. After allowing ample water to spray clean my nude body and scrubbing myself dry, with no shame, no pretense, naturally and joyously I went to Andy, who sat in a bathrobe on the side of the bed.

"Do you dare to come to me this way?" And he began christening me, as he would wish me, always, to be: "little baby" and then "my baby doll." I would forever after be his "baby doll."

We were in an iron-frame bed that was against a window, with glass panes that slid up and down. We listened as a rainstorm beat against the window, and we heard loud claps of thunder and saw a sky streaked with lightning. I knew earliest primitive people believed that when the rains descended the Male God who lived in the sky was pouring his fertile liquid onto Mother Earth. For me the thunder was big bass drums, the wind a high reed, wailing, "Let me in, let me in." With Andy I was giving, and giving is what makes that night memorable.

In time, we drove to a nearby town, got a license, had a church wedding and boarded the coach car of a train. I kept a record: "two pillows, fifty cents." We sat all the way to New York, where we attended the wedding of Andy's daughter, Jean, a librarian slightly older than I. Back in Fort Worth, life continued as before: we went to movies and danced at the casino, working, eating, amusing ourselves. Summing it all up I recall a line in a theatrical production about a couple who had lived happily, "for a little while." Later, when I would vow that I still loved Andy — though I now believe it was the idea of love that I loved — those to whom I made that vow would demand a reasonable, pragmatic answer as to why I left him. As I had not been able to give one to Andy, I could not provide it for others. "What happened?" An interlocutor would wait for an answer, a simple answer he or she might understand, expecting to hear the worst, such as he is not as he seems, in private he beats me or I had fallen out of love with him and into love with another. No, no, I would say, it was not that simple, and often I am sure Andy wished that it were. He was accustomed to a "right" and a "wrong," so where was the wrong? "Baby doll," he asked, "have I not 'loved' you enough?" He meant that in the physical sense, had he not performed the act of intercourse sufficiently often, and that seemed ironic since the physical more than the spiritual or mental aspects of life had brought us together and indeed been our main bond. After three years of marriage, the physical act was no longer sufficient bond for me. At the time I did not sort this out — I felt only guilt, pain, anguish.

One evening, as I was washing dishes and Andy preparing for bed, I suddenly began weeping and ran from the kitchen. To whom could I talk? Approaching a tree, I threw my arms around its strong trunk and rubbed my face against its rough bark. Tree, eternity, God, whatever you are, I don't want to settle for a kind of getting through life without having lived it. Give me a bigger plan, even if it involves hardships. I stopped the flow of tears, returned to the dishes. When I tried to talk to Andy, I could not find the right words. He looked perplexed:

"Baby doll, you seem 'mixed up.'" Andy felt the marriage was made in paradise, so what was wrong with me? "I am like an old horse, standing in the barn," Andy said. "I am the same, I did not change." And in truth, he had not, which he saw as a virtue.

We had a mutual friend, a retired district judge, in his eighties, to whom I confessed my restlessness, a fugitive itch to move on. "Grace," said the judge, giving me a wink, "next time find a man who will keep you barefoot and pregnant." That was a common joke. It was forever thought that a woman's primary function was to have children. In marrying Andy, I presumed we would have children, although we had not discussed the issue, a fact which in a more enlightened age strains credulity. In our sexual act, he used a condom, or before climax, withdrew from my body. "Why?" I asked. Andy explained how difficult it had been, putting two children through college on his meager salary. Since the breakup of his first marriage he had always taken measures to prevent a pregnancy, and he continued that practice with me. He was adamant about the issue. It was only when he realized he might lose me that he cried, "Let's have a baby!"

"Is it wise," I asked, "to use a child to keep us together?" If I had wanted a child above all else in this world, or even if I had wanted to preserve a marriage above all else in this world, I would have made the demand of him: let's get on with it. But neither of those purposes was my ultimate one.

A decade later, in another part of the world, I decided my role in life was not procreation. I did not need to sacrifice a nurturing instinct; I could care for many, become "a mother" to a multitude.

But initially I lacked that insight. I felt only inner conflict. My heart was saying go, while my mind was saying: settle for all that you possess, a nice home, a car, a secure future. On one hand I felt constricted, constrained, in a box. I wanted to expand, to include more wonder, poetry and music in my life. Still, I was burdened by guilt. Breaking the traditional mold was not the norm for a woman of my era, reared in a church atmosphere that taught one entered a marriage for better or worse, in short, for life.

I went to my father, then ninety-two:

"I don't know what to do."

"You made a decision to leave," he said. "Stick to it!" Again he was saying what he had told me at age five: "Daughter, you have a will, the power of the will."

I found it easier to weep than to search for "will." Often I wondered where it was located, maybe in my head or in my heels? How could I so easily cut clean from a marriage? Andy, I told my father, was a good man.

"Daughter," replied my father, who never dealt in pieties, "there is no disparity in marriage like unsuitability of mind and purpose."

One evening I told Andy: "I am leaving." We were standing in our kitchen. He grabbed a large butcher knife, placed the blade to my throat. "No!" he shouted. "I won't lose you! Stay — or I'll kill you!"

I felt a strange sense of not caring one way or the other what he did. It was like freedom. "Go ahead!" I dared. When Andy paused, I baited, "You don't have the nerve!" He dropped the knife and wept. A man's tears, coming from down deep.

In response to my guilt for leaving, I reasoned: Andy likes things, I will leave him all we have. And so I did. I left him our home and our bank account, all our possessions. I bought an airplane ticket to Paris and had only fifty dollars in my purse when I left, hoping to find who I was meant to be. In looking back, I see that leaving the marriage was the most difficult — and the most wise — of any of my decisions.

Years later a friend asked, regarding the big age difference between Andy and me: "Did you think you were 'marrying your father'?" And others have said, "You had a 'father complex.'" Even Andy once said, "You love your father more than you do me." As for loving my father more, which indeed was the case, Pascal reminds us that we can love only good qualities. Loving good qualities is quite apart from sexual attraction. I was sexually attracted to Andy. Such attractions, in my experience, always wane. But the good qualities in a person live on, in our lives, and this is the enduring "love" of which Pascal spoke.

PART

Travel

FOUR

7: New York: Meeting Women Role Models

*"Women should have liberty of experience; they should differ
from men without fear and express their difference openly...
all activity of the mind should be so encouraged that there will
always be in existence a nucleus of women who think, invent,
imagine, and create as freely as men do, and with as little fear
of ridicule and condescension."*
— *Virginia Woolf,* The Selected Letters of Virginia Woolf

In my two Texas newspaper jobs, in Lubbock from
1941 to 1943 and in Fort Worth from 1945 to 1952, I
saw no woman in a position of authority. In between those
two newspaper jobs, however, from 1943 to 1945, I lived
in New York. And there for the first time I began to meet
working women who became role models.

This was significant for me since I was born and grew up
in a time and place when a woman knew her place and
generally kept it. She was a stoker of the home fires, a nur-
turer for husband and children. Those who ventured into
a world outside the home found limited job opportunities,
such as store clerk, schoolteacher or secretary. Growing
up, I never saw a woman in a military uniform, a police-
woman, a woman driving a bus, a woman working in a
bank, a woman deacon, a woman on the city council. The
vast majority of women around me had not gone to college, were not widely traveled or read. They grew up
believing in one primary goal: finding a man to provide for

them. They were the second sex. Most were indoctrinated to believe they were not as intelligent, as worthy or equal to a man. Since we tend to become how others see us, most women felt themselves inferior to men.

I was twenty in 1943 when I left Lubbock for New York. To get there, I withdrew savings garnered from my *Avalanche-Journal* work and bought a coach ticket. After sitting up three days and four nights, I arrived at Grand Central and began sharing an apartment with my sister Hortense. Called the Juilliard, our apartment building was at Broadway and 122nd and was adjacent in that era to the famed Juilliard Music School.

Soon after my arrival, I boarded a streetcar, traveling down Broadway to 42nd Street. Disembarking, I walked a block to *The New York Times*, went to the personnel office and applied for a job. "There's an opening in our reference room," I was told. "You would help editorial writers find source material and also run their copy to a Linotype room." I accepted eagerly.

In my work I came to know, in a cursory way, a half dozen editorial writers who sat in private offices facing the reference room, among them Anne O'Hare McCormack, the first woman to write editorials for the *Times*. I was deeply impressed by her and her ability to write her own commentaries, wrapping up complex problems or situations in simple words the average reader could understand. Watching her at work, I felt she was doing what I would one day like to do: get the facts of a situation and use them in a manner that would go beyond mere data to some kind of "truth." McCormack, then in her forties, was a short woman who wore simple suits and sensible shoes, and while she was of serious demeanor, she also had an easy, winning smile. When I delivered research data to her, she would on occasion ask me about myself. Her comments gave me the impression she was seeing me and giving me stature as a person.

Some decades later, in the seventies and eighties, after I had written several books, I was invited to the home of Mrs. Arthur Hays (Iphigene) Sulzberger, who had been dubbed "the mother" of *The New York Times.* Her father started the paper. Later her husband, and still later on, her son ran the paper. Visiting her country home in Greenwich, Connecticut, I stood with her before a framed photograph of Anne O'Hare McCormack, and she told me about her husband's decision to hire her:

"At the time, it was most unusual for a big newspaper to permit a woman writer to express her own opinions in personal commentaries." In addition to McCormack, she could think of only one other woman in her league — Dorothy Thompson. Thinking of these women who spoke their own minds, Iphigene Sulzberger made a comment all too typical of millions of women: "As for me, I have never done anything — on my own. All my life I have stood in the shadow of a man — first my father, then my husband, later my son."

In my early days in New York, I met a second woman, Ruth Benedict, a professor at Columbia University, who also made a deep impression on me. The apartment where I lived was only four blocks up Broadway from Columbia University. At that time, the regular university curriculumwas restricted to males, but females were permitted to enroll in night classes. I chose a course in anthropology, with Benedict as the professor. She talked to us about the variety of physical and cultural characteristics of humankind. And it was through her lectures and assigned reading material that I first considered the manner in which pigmentation can be used as a means of discrimination. What she taught, stored in recesses of my mind, became the earliest seed of my decision twenty-five years later to change the color of my skin and write *Soul Sister.*

In New York, I went to my first symphony orchestra concert, to my first opera, to my first museums. For $1.10

I could sit in a top balcony and see the great dramas of Shakespeare, O'Neill, Ibsen, Tennessee Williams. I heard lines spoken by the greatest array of actors and actresses Broadway has known: Helen Hayes, Tallulah Bankhead, Cornelia Otis Skinner, Katherine Cornell, Lynn Fontaine and Alfred Lunt. In that era, actors did not have the use of microphones and other amplification devices. Yet, the great men and women of the theater so perfectly enunciated and projected their words that even from a top balcony I heard as clearly as if they were two feet removed.

New York at that time was a manageable, clean city, throbbing with excitement, and with easy, safe, cheap transportation. I traveled uptown or downtown or across town by streetcar or subway for five cents. For another five cents, I embarked on a Staten Island ferry, enjoying cool breezes while seeing Manhattan bathed in a myriad of lights. I traveled any place in New York, at any hour, day or night, without fear of robbery or assault.

Although I was living through a period of some of the most bitter fighting of the Second World War, I am amazed, in retrospect, at how little I knew or talked about the events that were occurring "over there." My sister and I did not own a television, it being a new invention, not widely used, nor did we listen to many radio broadcasts. Though my two brothers were engaged in the fierce struggle to defeat Nazism, the war seemed to be on another planet, other than when we got letters from those in combat.

In 1944, I moved from the *Times* reference room to become a writer on the news desk of the Office of War Information, at West 57th Street near Broadway. Now twenty-one, I was assigned by news editor Ted Kaghan to cover a luncheon with Mrs. Eleanor Roosevelt as speaker. I sat at a table quite close to her. At first glance, I had a typical cursory impression: her teeth protruded and were too big while her chin fell in layers. Once she began to speak, however, I saw a radiance that softened uneven features. I knew I was in the presence of a woman who was uniquely herself. Many Americans despised her, but I came to realize this was due in part to her strong opinions and perhaps even more to her assumption that she, a woman, had a right to speak her mind as freely as a man.

Some three decades after covering Mrs. Roosevelt's New York luncheon talk, I was invited to lunch to discuss "Mrs. R" by the *Times-Mirror*'s Martin Levin, who had published two of my early books. "There's a medical doctor here in New York," Levin began, "wants to write a book on his relationship with Mrs. Roosevelt. He was her personal physician and traveled with her on many of her overseas trips." Then he got to the point: "The doctor is no writer. Will you ghostwrite the book for him?"

I accepted Levin's proposal and began shuttling between Washington and New York. From LaGuardia Airport, I taxied to the doctor's flat at Fifth Avenue near 75th Street. I entered a brownstone, purchased by Mrs. Roosevelt, who had retained two floors while the doctor and his wife lived on another two floors. I interviewed and tape-recorded the doctor, with sessions beginning Friday afternoon and continuing, with various breaks, until Sunday afternoon. Returning to my Washington apartment, I transcribed the tapes and wrote a draft chapter. On the following Friday, I again shuttled to New York for more interviews.

The doctor's entire flat was a photo gallery with pictures of Mrs. Roosevelt in every available space. It was as if she were the only person he had ever known — she filled his life. And he talked about her nonstop. He had a compulsion to see himself as existing only in her light. For some weeks, I wrote chapters only to have him change his mind about what he had said in a previous one. He was confused. He wanted to give meaning to himself through the relationship, but what was this meaning? He implied by innuendos that they had known a sexual liaison, but when it became clear how much he wanted me to believe this, I became convinced it never happened.

On several occasions, after I had tape-recorded the doctor, I met in the evenings with Maureen Corr, who had been a secretary to Mrs. Roosevelt and who knew the doctor quite well. Did she, I asked Maureen over supper one evening, believe Mrs. R and the doctor ever had more than a platonic relationship? "Certainly not," she said. She speculated, as did I, that it was only if we believed that Mrs. Roosevelt "loved" him in a sexual way that he would gain stature, that this was the means by which others might imagine him as her peer.

After some months, Levin and I met for dinner, and both of us agreed: the doctor was turning into more of a problem than a project. We agreed to drop him.

Increasingly over the years I have realized how much Mrs. Roosevelt did to encourage women journalists. Herself a newspaper columnist, the First Lady resented male editors excluding most women reporters from covering news other than society. In 1963, when I came to Washington, men continued to exclude women from their press club membership. I joined the Women's National Press Club. In 1971, the club changed its name to the Washington Press Club and admitted men. Three days later, after almost three-quarters of a century, the all-male National Press Club admitted women for the first time. And in 1985, the two clubs merged. Certainly the relentless prodding by Eleanor Roosevelt encouraged white men to be more inclusive, to share their power with minorities and with women. Perhaps of all our First Ladies, she was the most talented, the most courageous. In her own right, she was a thinker, an achiever — a good role model for other women who seek individuation.

In 1945, after two years in New York, I returned to Texas, where I lived until I left Andy to begin my life freelancing around the world.

8: Europe: Free-Lancing and Looking for Texans

"Sing away sorrow, cast away care."
— *Cervantes,* Don Quixote

I was twenty-nine when I left my Fort Worth home, husband, a salaried job, all security. I had no credit cards, no bank account. Even Don Quixote had Sancho Panza, but I set out alone on my quest. I had a dream: to prove to myself I could start from scratch, travel the world and earn my living by the articles I sold. I now had eleven years of work experience, in Lubbock for two years, in New York for two years, and in Fort Worth for seven years. Additionally, for the *Star-Telegram*, I had made two short trips, in 1947 and 1951, to Europe.

In 1952, with the Second World War behind us, America was busy making friends of former enemies, while at the same time growing increasingly jittery about a former ally, the Soviet Union, which had disregarded its wartime agreements and taken over half of Europe. In addition to having American GIs on the battlefield in Korea, the United States had tens of thousands of U.S. men based throughout Europe, on the alert as a "cold war" threatened to become another world conflagration.

I studied the situation overseas and thought of a plan to sell stories to Texas editors. Borrowing my brother Harry's car, I drove from Fort Worth to El Paso —that's twelve

hundred miles round-trip. And midway I stopped in
Midland. On other days I drove to Dallas, Waco, Austin,
Houston. And I made still another trip to Lubbock and
Amarillo. Arriving at a newspaper office after a long drive
— it was a hot summer, and back then cars had no air-
conditioning — I went to a ladies' room to freshen up.
Then I asked to see the managing editor. Usually his door
was open. Seated before an editor with a serious though
friendly demeanor, I began:

"I'm going to Europe. I will look around for servicemen from your area." I suggested that his readers —
fathers, mothers, wives, sisters, brothers, friends of these
servicemen — would find my "hometown" features of
interest. In talking with an editor, such as R. J. Watts of
the *Houston Chronicle*, Felix McKnight of the *Dallas
Morning News*, Bill Collyns of the *Midland Reporter-
Telegram* or Harry Provence of the *Waco News-Tribune*,
I did not ask for a contract, advance or expense money,
nor did I inquire of any editor what he might pay for an
article. I asked only that he look at my copy, which they
all agreed to do.

When I boarded a propeller-driven plane for Paris, I had
a one-way ticket and five ten-dollar bills in my purse. "We
know God takes care of you," sighed my Fort Worth sister, adding, "but why do you make it so hard on Him?"
Landing around noon on September 20 and carrying a
small French-English dictionary, I asked directions to
SHAPE, the headquarters of the European command.
Boarding a designated bus, I arrived, after an hour's drive,
at the headquarters, which was like a small Pentagon, with
all nationalities of the NATO organization working side by
side. General Dwight Eisenhower had been succeeded in
that year by General Matthew Ridgway. With insouciance,
I approached a uniformed guard: "I want to see General
Ridgway." I had no appointment, I was not "cleared" to
see a general, yet the guard did not subject me to body

search or catechism. Rather, "Have a seat." And within minutes, "This way, the general will see you."

As VIPs in those days were not harassed by an army of adversarial reporters, the general acted pleased to receive me, treating me in a genial, avuncular manner. Politely answering my questions, he readily agreed to my snapping his picture. Soon the general was setting up appointments with other members of his staff and in particular with the Texans under his command.

As I moved about Europe, I met other American reporters and photographers, but they were all salaried employees. I met no other writer or photographer who was earning his or her keep as a free-lance writer. And no one seemed to understand how I kept afloat. "I've always thought free-lancing was writing mostly for free," said Tom Curran, European manager for the United Press wire service. "How do you make it pay?" I kept hearing the same query: how did I manage without a fixed salary? And that query echoed through the years: in 1995, Staley McBrayer, a veteran Texas newspaper publisher, said, "I always figured you were with the CIA. Otherwise, how could you have earned enough to travel so far?"

There were several reasons why my free-lancing technique worked for me: first, I was riding a wave of optimism. Americans generally believed we were a special people who could wrap up the wounds of war-ravaged Germany and France and Italy, build a better tomorrow, make the world safe for democracy. By the mid-nineties, President Bill Clinton told Americans he was weary of airwaves carrying "a constant, unremitting drumbeat of negativism and cynicism." When I set out, we were marching to a different drummer. We were risk takers, hopeful, energetic. Having won the war, we were embarked on a new period of great confidence, prosperity and change. We felt a part of the onward march of science, technology, manufacturing. Americans were building huge corporations, producing cars, refrigerators, radios, televisions that were the envy of the world. I was imbued with this can-do spirit and equipped with the energy that supreme optimism provides.

A second reason I could stay afloat: hometown stories sold well in Texas. When I sent the same type stories to the *Daily Oklahoman* and the *New Orleans Times-Picayune*, the editors were not interested. In contrast the Texas editors would print *any* story, provided it was about a Texan. And I found Texans everywhere. In every army, air force and navy base I visited, the Texans, from the lowest private to the highest-ranked general or admiral, posed proudly for pictures when told their photos would appear back home in Texas. Regardless of where I found them, the Texans, seeing my camera, produced from what appeared thin air huge silken Texas flags, as well as cowboy boots, Stetson hats and hometown newspapers.

My questions were no-brainers, such as, "What do you miss?" Or, "How do you like it over here?" However simplistic my query they responded in kind, with statements proving they were not overly impressed with Old World culture, edifices or charms but rather staying loyal to their one true love, the Texas Way of Life.

What did he think, I asked a Timpson, Texas, native, of Paris?

"It is not near as modern as I thought it would be."

Of a Texas sergeant, who had been stationed in Rome for four months, I inquired what historical sights had he seen?

"These old ruins, you mean? I don't go in for 'em."

Had he seen the Colosseum?

"That old stadium? Oh, I might have driven by the place, I dunno."

In Naples, where Byron had waxed poetic over a bay strung out like a necklace of pearls, a Houstonian insisted: "It's *nothing* compared to Galveston."

Where in all the world did he like best, I asked a Texan stationed at Bovingdon, England, who had returned from Istanbul, Athens, Rome and Paris.

"I prefer Bandera, Texas," he replied. "I like to go hunting in that neck of the woods."

In Fontainebleau, outside Paris, I visited a Dallas major, Jack A. Whitely, and his family, who lived in a house Chopin had shared with the famous woman writer George Sand. The home was still furnished with pianos, one upstairs and one downstairs, on which the composer had played. But the Texans didn't like the house. "The ceilings are too high." Neither the major nor his wife Mabel played the piano, except for photo purposes. As my camera clicked, the major, wearing his Stetson and cowboy boots, gave a rendering of "Chopsticks."

In Nancy, France, I trudged through rain and mud interviewing servicemen bundled in woolens, but a private from Laredo, dressed in khaki, avowed he couldn't move "in all those layers" and somehow managed to wear his khakis all year round. Then there was the Texan in Berlin with two wristwatches: "So I'll always know what time it is in Texas."

A third reason I managed to keep traveling through France, Germany, Italy, Belgium, Holland, Spain, Yugoslavia and even beyond: the U.S. dollar was king, as sound as Gibraltar. With only a few dollars, I could register in any European hotel, eat in any restaurant. Once, cashing a sixty-dollar check from Midland's Bill Collyns, I went to a German tailor, chose fine worsted wool, paid for a hand-tailored suit and still had dollars to spare.

Most editors paid an average of fifteen dollars per story. By changing the lead to give a hometown slant that would be special for each paper, I often sold the same story to four, five or even six different editors, which meant I garnered as much as ninety dollars for one story. Also, as an accredited correspondent with the Pentagon, I could stay

in hotels requisitioned by the U.S. military, such as the
Schwartzerbach in Wiesbaden, the Excelsior in Munich or
the Bristol in Vienna, for one dollar a night. And I could
eat in U.S. mess halls for as little as fifty cents. Additionally,
I could fly "space available" on U.S. cargo planes. Along
with a few servicemen, I sat in so-called bucket seats made
of steel and attached to the sides of the aircraft. The planes
were not heated. It was on such aircraft that I flew into
Izmir, Turkey, and U.S. air bases then operating in Tripoli,
Libya and Dhahran, Saudi Arabia.

Often I benefitted from a kind of reverse discrimination.
Once, in England, along with other correspondents, I
boarded a U.S. Navy plane to reach the Greek island of
Zante, which had suffered near total devastation from an
earthquake. We flew to Araxos on the mainland of Greece,
where we awaited a seaplane. Spotting the arrival of the
smaller craft, I feared I'd be bumped. Around me were
VIPs with large readerships, including Carl Mydans, the
famed *Life* photographer, as well as AP and UP reporters,
covering for outlets throughout the world, and Howard
Smith of CBS.

I noted the men — I was the only woman among them
— shoving one another to board the plane. Nearby I saw
the pilot, who had left the cockpit momentarily to stretch
his legs. I introduced myself and got a broad smile from
First Lieutenant Leonard Sweet, who quickly volunteered
he was from Texas. As for my getting aboard, "Don't
worry," he assured me, "I won't leave without you! Even
if the plane is full, we'll make room." Beyond the fact that
we were both Texans and that my readership could include
his family members, I enjoyed special privileges because I
represented "womanhood," and in that era, this was a status to be protected, respected and honored. Lieutenant
Sweet handed me a life jacket. I climbed aboard and lay flat
in a narrow berth. After we were all strapped in, the Texan
revved the motors and we took off.

After a smooth landing on water, the correspondents clamored onto the island of Zante, where we discovered every building, save one, had been destroyed. I noted that Mydans and I were using Rolleiflex cameras. He seemed never to stop clicking. "Get a hundred shots," he shouted to me, sharing his secret of success. "One will surely be good!"

In West Berlin, I saw my first helicopter. Wandering around Tempelhof air base, I met a Lieutenant Leggett of Fort Worth who was working on a whirlybird. It appeared little more than a toy, but since it had space for two, I asked about getting a ride: "How about East Berlin?" It was then under communist rule.

"With these new parts," he said, pointing to an unopened package, "we should be able to stay airborne." Handing me a man's flight suit, he pointed to a sign, "Men's Latrine." While I changed, he installed the new parts. Then, with no authorization from his superiors, I climbed aboard. Strapping myself in, I was startled by Leggett literally yanking doors off their hinges. "You'll see better," he explained, laying the doors aside.

He climbed into pilot's position, and we fluttered upward. Soon I looked down on the Brandenburg Tor, the dividing line between the communist East and the West sectors. The blade was whirling loudly as we circled over thousands of East Germans congregated for a rally and a parade of "Free German Youths." Amazed by the mysterious whirlybird over their heads, the marching youths stopped in their tracks, craning their necks and staring at us as they would a flying saucer. Above the roar, I shouted to Leggett that he had startled the youths and stopped their parade.

"They've never seen a 'chopper.' They are new, even to us." He added that in all of Europe, "the air force has only two and the army only three." Then realizing where we were and the value of the small craft: "We better get out of here," he said. "The Russians would like to get their hands on this 'bird.'"

At the Erding Air Depot in southern Germany, I sought a story on "Operation Christmas," a project in which U.S. military men personally bought and wrapped gifts for four hundred German orphans. Might I go along, I asked a Texas lieutenant, for the gift distribution? "All right," he agreed. Then, grinning, he added, "But you have to be Santa Claus!" He handed me an oversized red suit and a white beard. I dutifully found a men's latrine and got suited.

After we roared straight up, then leveled off, he produced a picture postcard, shouting, "This is what the orphanage looks like. I've never been there. Now you navigate." We flew to Wartenberg, and, near a large church shown on my postcard "map," I spotted the orphanage. In our vertical descent, I watched the town's waiting dignitaries break rank and run to avoid the dust we churned up. After we were safely planted on level ground, the mayor and others gathered around us. The dignitaries and the hundreds of orphans registered surprise to find a St. Nicholas in high heels and calling out names in a twangy Texas accent. But they were far more curious about our machine that had come straight down from the skies. None of them had ever seen a whirlybird.

On another day, at Rhein-Main in Frankfurt, I climbed into the cockpit of a cargo plane to fly within a seventeen-mile corridor on the famed Berlin Air Lift route. I sat between two pilots, one a Texan named Miller. "Russian MiGs often come alongside us and fly formation," said Miller, who had flown 225 delivery trips. We were on the route inaugurated in 1948 when American C-47s began a twenty-four-hour schedule proving to the world that America would not desert its hold in Berlin.

As we neared Tempelhof, the weather closed in. The pilots and I could see nothing ahead but a black "soup." I listened as a U.S. serviceman in a tower talked us down with a ground control approach (GCA): "You are thirteen miles out. Descend to three thousand feet." Soon, out of the darkness I saw an orderly row of landing strip lights stretching before the nose of the C-47. With a perfect landing, we ended another successful flight of "Operation Vittles," a program in which U.S. airmen flew 109,228,502 miles, the equivalent of 227.8 trips to the moon, and delivered 2,324,257 tons of food and materials to a blockaded city.

Fighting wars and keeping the peace were considered, back in my era, to be men's responsibilities. There were only a few women in uniform. At all the military installations I visited, if I asked the commanding officer to round up the Texans, he produced for my interviews only males. In Wiesbaden, on my own, I found one of America's most famed aviators, Captain Helen Wheeler. She had owned her own airport in Palestine, Texas, had instructed hundreds of air force men and navy cadets how to fly at Prescott, Arizona, as well as movie stars including Jimmy Stewart, Robert Taylor and Mary Astor. She was the first woman commissioned after the air force became a separate branch of the armed forces. During the Second World War she ferried planes to various bases in the United States and Canada. She had piloted everything from single-engine lightweights to four-motored heavy bombers. In Wiesbaden, I found her in the air force's mail and records section. Did she still fly? I asked her. Did she still teach? "No, I got 'grounded.'"

But why?

"When the war ended, they told me flying was a man's job." If there were few women pilots, there were also few women working in city newsrooms. In the late thirties, Hope Ridings Miller from Texas worked as the only woman on the *Washington Post* city news staff. "I knew no discrimination," she frequently recalled. "I was treated courteously at all times by every man on the staff. The veteran city news editor, John Riseling, went out of his way to give me assignments that earned me my share of by-lines."

But were not women such as the two of us benefitting from a reverse discrimination, being treated like Meissen china simply because we were rare? And being rare meant that we had managed to slip through the barriers that kept most others out. When Miller was making her name covering the Washington diplomatic scene, hundreds of other women writers undoubtedly would have liked to work on the *Post.* Yet it would be some decades before they would find job opportunities. To say of the early days, "I made it, I knew no discrimination," means only that being one of a kind, *one* single woman working among men, represented no real threat to the men who had enough competition, they felt, from other men. In fact, by making a success in a man's world and in such an early period, women such as Miller and I might be likened to a dog walking on his hind legs: the wonder was not that the dog did so well but that it was done at all.

9: Japan and Hong Kong: Had I Ever Wished to Be Born a Man?

"The females must obey the males."
—*Lafcadio Hearn*, Japan: An Attempt at Interpretation

For me, the Orient was always under a veil, in a remote, misty distance. Since it appeared mysterious and inaccessible, it loomed more desirable. I wondered how I might get there. How might I identify with people who do not look like me and perhaps do not have the same thought patterns? What might I learn from them? I had sold stories from Europe. Could I do the same in the Orient? Determined to go, I felt like Sir Edmund Hillary, who, asked why he scaled Mount Everest, replied "because the mountain is there."

In 1955, I bought a one-way Pan-Am ticket to Japan. I boarded a propeller-driven airplane and flew some ten hours. After an overnight in Hawaii, I continued on the next day. And on and on. I lost track of days, but eventually, in a deluge of rain and knowing no one, I put my feet on Japanese soil. I arrived ten years after the U.S. had dropped atomic bombs on two of Japan's main cities. Yet, I was not thinking about my nation being the first to "nuke" another. In fact, it would be decades before I, like other Americans, dredged from the recesses of my mind the fact that we had bombed not army camps but cities, killing civilian men, women and children. At the time, Americans were told the deed was done "to save lives," meaning the lives of U.S. soldiers who, had the Japanese not surrendered, otherwise could have been killed. Like most Americans, I had been indoctrinated during wartime to see the Japanese as bad people. We found it easier to hate them than the Germans. It has been suggested that since the Nazis had white skin and looked like white Americans, the U.S. would never have dropped atom bombs on them. On the other hand, I have thought that it caused little soul-searching for white Americans to drop them on dark-skinned Asians.

Originally, I had planned to stay a week. But I could get no reading on how I felt. Did I dislike the people? But how could I like or dislike until I got to know them as individuals? After a few days' stay at the Imperial Hotel, designed by Frank Lloyd Wright—its "floating foundation" made it one of the few Tokyo structures to withstand a 1928 earthquake—I moved to a typical Japanese inn. Here I began to acquaint myself with floors of soft straw *tatami* mats for simple living by day and sleeping at night. I ate bean-curd soup and raw fish for breakfast. Each night, after first scrubbing myself clean outside the *ofuro*, I plunged my body into scalding hot waters, a bathing ritual that parboils the skin and relaxes one from tensions of a stressful day.

Beyond writing articles for stateside publications, I also wanted a "home base" job where I would feel, to some extent at least, a part of the society in which I was living. With this in mind, I applied for a job at the *Nippon Times*. The newspaper, later called the *Japan Times*, was one of four English-language dailies published in Tokyo. I was lucky in that tens of thousands of Japanese, as well as a large number of English-speaking foreigners, bought such newspapers. The Japanese editor hired me to write a daily column, entitled "Around Tokyo." I began to meet Japanese and in time I came to know Akiho-san, a singular woman, struggling to break from a traditional mold of "doll" women who lived their lives in service of men.

Akiho-san was twenty-five and petite. Standing about five feet, she dressed simply, in western style, with dark hair pulled back from her face. She was one of an exceedingly small number of Japanese women, and the only one I came to know, who in the mid-fifties was attempting to live entirely on her own. She had a job that paid the equivalent of twenty-five dollars a month as a commercial artist for the Canon Photography Company, one of countless Japanese companies then gearing up that in time would mushroom into international commercial giants.

When I asked if I might stay awhile in Akiho-san's tiny flat, she was surprised by the request but welcomed me. I entered a minuscule rectangular box, not as large as many U.S. walk-in closets. The floor, typically, had *tatami* mats. A wall shelf held a hotplate. On another wall I saw two shelves for clothes and bedding. At night we lay on the *tatami* mats, our heads near one wall, our legs in close proximity to another. Her flat had no heating of any kind, and, to help keep warm, each of us slept in layers of clothing. For meals, we used the hotplate to make rice or noodles and cups of hot tea. I learned how Akiho-san made a budget: "I pay four thousand yen for rent." That was eleven dollars. She also budgeted eleven dollars a month for food. That left three dollars for miscellaneous expenses.

Going to a public bath cost ten yen, less than three cents. We first entered a cold room with bare floors and a temperature about freezing. Shucking our clothes, we moved to a steam-filled room where we diligently scrubbed all parts of our bodies. Then we proceeded to a community pool of hot water, used by both men and women. None of the Japanese seemed shy about bathing together in the nude. To wash our hair, we went to a separate area and paid four cents.

Once, we were eating bowls of rice in her flat and Akiho-san turned to me with a serious, sad expression: "Have you ever felt that woman is unhappy?" she asked. "Here we have almost no rights. We are expected to get married, to care for a husband. He has to come first, always. And it is simple for a Japanese man to divorce his wife. That costs him, in your money, only twenty-eight cents. A man who wants a divorce need not state a reason. He does not need to wait, he faces no complications, no court procedure. So a wife is totally vulnerable. Often she is married to a man she has not previously known. That was the case with my mother. My mother always told me, 'A woman's lot is harder than man's. It is our fate. Only evil will come if we protest against it.' I always heard that, from my earliest childhood."

How, I asked, had she escaped this bondage?

"Only because my father, who survived the war, later died of a heart attack."

"And if your father had lived, would he have permitted you to leave home?"

"No," she said. "I would not have escaped his domination. He would have forced me to marry a man of his choice." Authority, she added, meant everything to the Japanese. One's happiness was not an individual quest. "I was taught that a woman's happiness depends upon her duty to a male-dominated family, to a male-dominated nation."

I also came to know Chieko-san, whom I met on my first visit to Tokyo's Associated Press office, then headed by the American journalist Bob Eunson. Chieko-san worked as a receptionist. A slender, twenty-five-year-old attractive woman, Chieko-san dressed in a business suit and black high-heel pumps. Like Akiho-san, she spoke good English. She was reading Kafka, and, in describing the convoluted text, her beautiful brown eyes, large for Japanese eyes, turned extremely sad. In time, after many meetings for tea or lunch, or going to a dressmaker together, she began to talk about her father:

"He was one of the officials who had governed Korea while it was a Japanese war possession. After Japan's defeat in the big war, he was stripped of his authority and wealth. I would like to invite you to my home, but I cannot because of my father. It is not because he dislikes Americans," she said, perhaps not wanting to hurt my feelings, "but Father has his pride and does not want others to see how we live now."

One day, on a rocketing subway in the midst of Tokyo's chaotic rush hour, Chieko-san unexpectedly blurted out: "Have you not always wished you had been born a man? Women count for nothing!" I looked in silence around us: we were surrounded by dozens of female Japanese who did menial labor, babies strapped to their backs, their faces lined, their hands hardened by their chores. Having worked all day outside the home, they were en route to a second, demanding job: cooking and caring for husbands and children. Chieko-san seemed light-years removed from their plight. Yet, she felt her own role difficult.

"Always, all my life, I have hated being a woman. My older brothers always got the attention, the love. When I was growing up, if my father was asked, 'How many children do you have?' he would say 'three,' indicating he had three sons. I was not counted. In all instances, females must obey the males, first their fathers, then their husbands." As she continued talking above the din of the subway noises, my mind lingered on her initial query: had I not always wished I had been born a man? I realized that I had never wished that. And why was I different from this young Asian woman? Why did her father count his sons and make a cipher of her? Why must the girls in a family be servants to men — first the father, then a husband, then a son? Because my father had not seen me as a cipher, I did not discount her story. How many women were like Chieko-san, struggling against the greatest odds to find a voice? Until they found a voice, who would speak for them?

Everywhere in the Orient, I became aware of women who lived in conditions little better, physically, than the Stone Age. From Japan I eventually moved to Hong Kong, where I checked into the elegant Peninsula Hotel. I looked out my window, onto a nearby construction site. There I saw a Chinese woman breaking stones with a hammer, working as a laborer. No one was near her. Suddenly she lay down and gave birth to a baby. She cleaned the child, did the necessary tying of cords and, bundling her infant onto her back, continued her task of breaking stones. I had one thought: she was any woman. I could have been in her shoes. But then I could not have done what she, in her circumstances, was forced to do. Her "glass ceiling," the limit of her job opportunities, was no higher than the ground.

I later moved to the Foreign Correspondents Club, halfway up a spectacular mountain known as The Peak, locale for many of the scenes in the movie, *Love Is a Many Splendored Thing*. Every day, from the balcony of my room, I saw dozens of large, stately Chinese fishing junks with sails unfurled plying out to sea. What, I wondered, would it be like to live on one for awhile? I talked this over with Luis Bolero, a desk clerk at the Peninsula, with whom I had kept in contact after leaving the hotel. In his late twenties and unmarried, Bolero told me his father was Portuguese—the Portuguese had conquered the nearby island of Macao—and his mother Chinese. Luis spoke flawless English, as well as Portuguese and Chinese.

Once, as he and I looked at a Chinese junk sailing out to sea, I told him I had a dream to go live awhile on such a vessel. "It shouldn't be a problem," he said. "I'll talk with some fishermen." Some days later he called, said he had good news, and we met for tea. "I've found a junk and it's ready to sail. They'll take you," he told me. Before I could ask for details of where to go and what to take, Bolero began talking of his Chinese mother: "She represents my fondest childhood memories. But she died when I was ten. Still I remember her well. Most of all, I remember her taking me fishing in a sampan. Sometimes we would be away from shore for days. I loved that. It was a time when I had my mother, all to myself. And those memories, being on the water, just the two of us, are what she left me."

Because of those fond memories, he said he'd like to go along on the junk. "I can get some days off and be your interpreter." I readily agreed, as otherwise I would have had to communicate with the Chinese by sign language. On the appointed day, he and I set out, feeling our lives had just begun. We carried little gear. I wore slacks, blouse and sweater. We rode a bus to Castle Peak Bay where, after a short walk, we stepped onto the junk. The owner, a Mr. Chou, who was slightly built, in his fifties, with only a few teeth, greeted us: "Fishing won't be so good. This water is so sweet you can almost drink it." As Chou and Luis talked in Chinese, I was counting people: nineteen living on this junk, ranging from an infant to a friendly, energetic grandmother.

Setting sail, we moved out among other junks, sampans and ocean-going luxury liners. At sea, Chou showed Luis and me official papers from both the British, who controlled Hong Kong island, and from communist Chinese governments. "Inspectors from both these governments come aboard, every few days," he said, adding that inspections were frequent because when fishing was not good and an opportunity presents itself to carry cargo, "we do a little smuggling." I wondered, since he had announced fishing would not be good, if we were carrying narcotics or other banned goods.

For meals, we crouched in a circle on the deck and ate rice three times a day. The main cook was Chou's sister, who was named Ling and was obviously heavy with child. Each day, family members tossed out fishing nets and then brought them in, usually with no real catch, only tiny white fish no larger than a small finger. After Ling plunged them in steaming water, we devoured them heads and all. One day, we were lucky in landing large and succulent crabs, and these Ling steamed and served with rice.

I saw that throughout the operation the women handled the same equally difficult tasks as men. Two sisters, nineteen and twenty-one, used buckets to empty water that seeped into one of the bulkheads. I stayed on the junk for a week, and on the third day at sea, Ling, who had cooked all our meals, gave birth to her sixth child. Giving birth to a child apparently warranted no special privileges. The next morning, I noted, she was back at her kitchen chores.

While I was on the junk, the weather was warm, and each night Luis and I, along with the Chou family, slept in our clothes, on the open deck. I relished the simplicity of stretching out on a wooden deck, looking at the stars, feeling the gentle breezes, the rocking of the old junk and the Chinese lulling me to sleep with their soft Cantonese voices. As I shared the stars and the sea and the hard floor with the Chinese around me, I contrasted their lives to mine. I would return to live on the land, but this family had never known what it was like to live on terra firma. All of them were born on a junk, and, in the case of Chou, he told us, "I never step on land more than twenty times in a year." And when he does, "it is only for a brief time, to buy supplies." In that era, the Chou family was representative of two hundred and fifty thousand Chinese who were then living in junks and sampans in the Hong

Kong harbor, all of them born and all of them destined to die on their vessels.

By staying awhile with a family whose lifestyle was so different from my own, I gained new insights on my own life. Who was the person they were seeing? Was I all that different or did they only think that I was? The women touched the material in my clothing. I wore synthetics, different from loose-fitting cotton pants and tops, all black, that both men and women wore. They were curious about my having less pigmentation than they. And since all the Chinese females, even small babies, had their ears pierced, they were curious why I did not. The women told Bolero they thought it "most strange" that I traveled the world alone.

Living on the junk, I came to see how free I was compared with the Chou family, what infinite possibilities I had for travel, study, literature, art, music, all that was missing in their lives. Yet no one has it all. And I knew they had certain psychological cushions that I did not: they were born in a family that stayed together, living all lives close to one another and providing each other ballast. And, in contrast, I was attempting to paddle my own small boat on a very high sea.

10: Peru and Mexico: Latinos Speaking Up for Joy

"I find myself traveling for self-revelation; I reveal myself to myself in transit."
—*Russell Banks,* Continental Drift

In 1959, I was in New York and spotted an ad. The S.S. *Argentina* sailed in three days for Buenos Aires. I called and booked passage. Checking out of the Plaza Hotel, with one suitcase in hand, I hailed a taxi. I gave the number of a pier to the Irish driver, a Mr. McGrory. "And who, my dear," he asked, "will be seeing you off?"

"You! You!" I exclaimed. At the pier, I paid, tipped and, brimming with joy at a new sense of discovery, embraced Mr. McGrory. Then I walked aboard ship, bound for a new world. But, some friends asked later, why would you want to do that? And alone? I search for logical answers but always end up thinking my madness is right, their desire for a mundane security wrong. Would they say Columbus should have stayed put? Or Magellan? Or that Freya Stark, who in our current era explored places where no other Europeans had been, should have stayed home in England? Like Stark, a desire to know, to see with my own eyes, burns within me. Initially I am not always sure why I go one place and not another. As a writer, living my research, I trust my own vision, ears and heart.

The *S.S. Argentina* was so luxurious it was like the Waldorf Astoria afloat. After ten days, with stops in Rio de Janeiro and Montevideo, we docked in Buenos Aires. I checked into the Plaza of that grand city, and, after some days of baby beef and tangos, I moved on to Paraguay. Nothing much was going on there, except I discovered a land of beautiful flowers and beautiful people. I continued on to Bolivia, where, landing in the La Paz airport, I was at the height of Pikes Peak and looking up to the snow-capped Illimani Mountain rising more than twenty-one thousand feet. From La Paz I traveled to Lake Titicaca. Boarding a ship, I steamed across the highest navigable waters in the world, on a lake so large it took all night to traverse. And then I was in Peru. It was downhill from there, traveling by train over some of the most rugged and spectacular scenery this side of Nepal. Once at the Peruvian capital and settled in the Hotel Bolivar, I heard an inner voice saying: "Yes, you are lonely here. But stay. Find a place and live awhile."

The little house was there, where I looked for it, in the beautiful section of Lima called Miraflores, literally meaning, "look at the flowers."

Another day, I entered a building on Union Street, walked up a flight of stairs, entered the editorial offices of *La Prensa*, a Spanish-language daily owned by a Peruvian, Pedro Beltran. I had learned he was married to an American, Miriam, from San Francisco, who worked part-time at the paper. It was my good luck she was in her office. Meeting her, I said I wanted a job. But, unfortunately, my knowledge of Spanish was not sufficient to write in that language.

"I'd like to start a column for you in English," I proposed. Having researched the population, I cited the number of Lima residents who spoke English as their first language, as well as the number of Peruvians studying English "who will read my column, to practice their English."

"It sounds like a good idea," she agreed. Then we settled on my pay. That same day I handed city editor Pedro Cortazar a "Lima Today" column. Later I returned and read proof. I had absolute control over my material, such as the persons I chose to interview, and no editor ever changed my copy. I wrote a total of 1,095 columns for *La Prensa*—one a day for three years. During that time, 1959 to 1963, I traversed the length of the Peruvian coast, as arid as the sands of Saudi Arabia. I went on a whaling vessel off the coast from Paita and watched men shoot whales. This was before a worldwide moratorium, when men were shooting two thousand whales a year, some of them babies. I discovered the beauty of the Callejon de Huayas, with its nearly twenty-two-thousand-foot peaks and the all-white city of Arequipa.

One day I heard about a Peruvian engineer who would cross the Andes by jeep. I arranged to meet him and asked: might I go along? "Porque no?" Why not? he replied, and for reasons not quite clear he broke into laughter.

Jorge Carranza, thirty-eight, wore khaki pants and shirt. His face seemed half-hidden by thick horn-rimmed glasses. "I'll be on a business trip that will take me to the end of the road in Pucallpa," he explained. That would put us in the heart of the jungle. And it would be up to me to get back to civilization on my own. I nodded eagerly, and we left early the next morning from the Peruvian capital, which is at sea level. We began a rapid ascent. Only one hundred miles from Lima, we were at an altitude of 15,806 feet. In the mining town of Cerro de Pasco, made famous for its fabulous lodes of gold, silver, lead, zinc and copper, I saw young Peruvians playing soccer at fourteen thousand feet. After passing open pit mines, we soon began a rapid descent, racing along as on a roller coaster. We were leaping over deep gaps in the road. At every turn I felt we were plunging headlong into a canyon. Death-over-a-curve seemed first to await us on my right, then a sharp turn and there was a deathtrap on my left. Carranza seemed to think near-death was a joke as he spent much of his time in laughter.

"Don't worry!" he shouted, again breaking into laughter. "A witch doctor promised my mother: no accidents until I'm forty-eight!" I hoped her promise also included me. "We Latinos are fantastic people. Don't worry! Don't worry!" Then came more laughter. After eighteen hours on the road, we pulled into the settlement of Tingo Maria, where the Huallaga and Monzon rivers form a junction, which in an Indian dialect is "Tingo." It was midnight. We registered at a small hotel, with thatched roof. On the second day, we traveled from Tingo Maria to the end of the road at Pucallpa, with a climb over the watershed, the Blue Cordillera, between the Huallaga and Ucayali rivers.

All along the way, I enjoyed a great renewal, a great sense of discovery, as if my eyes were seeing the vastness of the universe for the first time. I felt enhanced, a part of the grandeur that filled me with rapturous, physical delight. Everywhere I saw beauty — butterflies as large as birds and sudden outbursts of flowering trees. We passed many waterfalls as spectacular as Yosemite in California. All around me was a new world, in every sense of the word: mountains still forming, rivers that don't know where they will go tomorrow. Wild, awesome, untamed — much of it as it was in the beginning of time.

Near our destination, Carranza and I began to pass over the worst section of the road. All truck traffic was barred. We were in a torrential rainstorm. The road in front of us looked like long strips of molasses. "It's slick, like driving on soap," Carranza admitted. We plowed and slipped, but he miraculously kept the jeep upright on one of the most arduous routes in the world. Although our second day's journey was only 185 miles, it was after midnight when we stopped at a small hotel. I took off my shoes, waded ankle-

"For a woman the act of creation is
prototypically to produce children."
          —Adrienne Rich, American poet

to another church for whites, he eventually released us. Perhaps more than anyone else I had met, Pearl seemed to me a black who would help change a racist America or die trying.

On another day, in the town of Clarksdale, I again went to a state employment office. I filled out an application for work as a maid. Back in those days that was about the only opening for a black woman. After my name was called, I sat for an interview with a woman clerk who produced the name of a white family, Wheeler. "They want someone for housecleaning, washing and ironing." I agreed to take the job, then stood on a street corner. Eventually Mrs. Wheeler, in a car of a designated color, arrived, and we drove to her home. I already had learned, from the employment agency, that her husband owned a large supply store where Mrs. Wheeler worked, and Wheeler himself was an important official in a Clarksdale bank.

Once inside her two-story colonial home, Mrs. Wheeler, dressed for her job at the office, remained only long enough to outline my chores: clean the commode, clean the tub, clean the floors, run the sweeper, wash clothes, do the ironing. Then she departed in her Impala. A daughter, Melissa, seventeen, breezed by. "Are you going to be permanent?" Not waiting for an answer, she hurried out and drove off in what was apparently her own car. The sudden departure of Mrs. Wheeler and then Melissa gave the house an air of impermanence. I walked to Melissa's bedroom, which was a shambles: panties left where she'd stepped out of them, bra on the floor nearby, slip there, shoes here, empty Cokes amid an assortment of dolls. Cleaning Melissa's room, making her bed, sorting her scattered clothing and realizing how little regard she had for her expensive dresses, I wondered how she would cope in a time and place where maids did not come cheap. From Melissa's room, I tackled the master bedroom, then a bedroom suite for Mr. Wheeler's blind mother, now away in a hospital, and a large den, as well as two baths, large kitchen, dining room and living room.

I ran a sweeper, dusted furniture and was in the midst of bringing in sheets from a clothesline, where they had dried in the sun, when I noticed that a car different from Melissa's or Mrs. Wheeler's was pulling into the drive. I presumed the current arrival to be Mr. Wheeler.

I was folding and sprinkling water on sheets and pillow-cases preparatory for ironing when Mr. Wheeler, in his late forties, with a receding hairline, entered the kitchen. Of medium build, he had soft body muscles that come from long hours of sitting. I did not look at him directly but kept my eyes on the laundry. Yet I sensed he was staring at me, and in that moment of silence, I felt he was somehow magnetized.

"What is your name? How long have you been here in Clarksdale?" He spoke in a businesslike manner, almost as if he were appraising a piece of jewelry. At the same time I noted a proprietary familiarity about his manner, as if he might be viewing me as a newly acquired household object. "You want to work here permanently?" In his rapid barrage he indicated he expected only cursory answers to perfunctory questions, leaving me with the sense that he was incapable of seeing me other than as a sexual object. I wondered how many other maids had stood in his kitchen, being so appraised. Relieved to see him abruptly walk from the room, I continued my work. Suddenly, from his mother's suite, came a thunderous clap. Had the blind woman's fish bowl fallen from its stand? Simultaneously, Wheeler was shouting: "Come quick!"

Hurrying upstairs, I had walked swiftly into the bed-room when the door slammed behind me. Turning around, I found myself encircled in Wheeler's arms, momentarily overwhelmed. He pressed his mouth roughly against mine and forced his body against me, muttering hoarsely about his desperate need for "black pussy." He already had unzipped his trousers, indicating he intended few if any preliminaries. His muscles strained against me, and he used his arms like a vise to prevent my breaking away. "Only take five minutes, only take five minutes," he mumbled, partly pleading, partly threatening. "Now quiet down! Gotta get me some black pussy!"

Although my arms were pinioned, I tried frantically to break his hold, and in the struggle we fell awkwardly onto the bed near the headboard. After he crawled on top of me, I felt myself suffocating from his body weight and panting breath. Somehow I wriggled free, jumped from the bed, attempting to flee, but again he grabbed me, pinning me against a wall, pushing me practically through the woodwork. He was holding me under a huge and ghastly oil painting of the entire family, in an ornate frame that must have weighed fifty pounds. Gaining use of one arm, I reached up and, with the last of my strength and willpower, I shoved the picture from its moorings. It came careening down. I had pushed it forward so that in its fall it grazed the back of Wheeler's head.

"You black bitch!" he cried, shaking with anger. His flushed face had dissolved from lust into hatred. More menacingly he added, his voice lowered to a whisper, "I ought to kill you, you black bitch!"

Suddenly, hearing the loud striking of a grandfather clock in the bedroom, he stepped aside. Perhaps it had reminded him that his wife and daughter were due home soon and that, unless he had time to rehang the picture, which he could not as the frame was now broken, some explaining would be in order. Seeing him momentarily stunned, I dashed downstairs and ran from the house. I maintained the pace for several blocks. Aware that I could not think straight, I only knew I must keep moving. Yet, when a police car cruised by, I slowed to a leisurely walk, pretending I knew where I was going in order to keep from attracting attention. Now I knew a fresh worry: had

Wheeler called the cops to get his revenge? Would he charge me with having stolen personal property? Have me locked up? Would they even allow me to use a telephone?

At an intersection I spotted a rattling 1960 sedan carrying a group of blacks. Running up, I blurted, "I've had an emergency" and asked if they would give me a lift into town. The family, a father, mother and three young children, made room for me, asking no questions. Surrounded by blackness I breathed more freely, certain that I was in the embrace of those who would be a protective shield. Their sympathy made Wheeler's "whitey world" bearable for the moment, and while they did not know what had happened, their instincts told them enough.

Back in the home of a black family where I was staying, I heated a pan of water to bathe my body. How many black women, I wondered, have worked all day for white people and never been paid for their labor, never been paid except as I was paid, by an insult, a threat to kill for not bowing before a white man's desires. If he had called the police, if I were interrogated, if he had said I stole a ring, what recourse would I—or the average black woman—have had? If it came down to a question of her "black" word against his "white" one? And why, my thoughts raced on, could he have been so certain that five minutes of lust for forbidden fruit would be his for the taking? In what depths of contempt he must hold all black women. True, the white man had used and often willy-nilly "taken" white women, but in the white woman-white man relationship there always was some reciprocity, she being the mistress of his home, the recognized mother of his children. Society in a sense was a protector to some degree of the white woman. But the black woman was totally vulnerable.

At the time Wheeler attempted to assault me, I tried to imagine my actually being a black woman with a black husband. Could I have told my husband of color: "That white man tried to rape me?" Then what? What could one black man have done against the entire system? Would one black man have had the nerve to take a gun and shoot the white man? Black men essentially had been castrated, made impotent—stripped of any power to defend their wives, daughters and sisters. Back in the sixties, they knew to "keep their place."

I began to see the role of the black woman in Wheeler's home objectively: she was me, and she was not me, because I could escape. But suppose a black woman in Wheeler's frenzied embrace had been a mother of hungry children, waiting for her to bring them food. Could she have resisted his advances? Run from the home without collecting any money for her day's labor? And suppose Wheeler had proved his claim—"Only take five minutes...only five minutes"—what might those five minutes have meant to an overburdened mother?

Suppose he had made a black woman pregnant. The child would be her child, not his! For his five minutes of sensuality she would pay for the rest of her life. The child, no matter how "fair" its skin, would be called a black. The mother would be struggling to buy food and to pay the rent, sacrificing to give the child even a second-rate education. And Wheeler? He would be at the bank appraising loans, in the church passing the collection plate, in the White Citizens Council making reports on the crime and violence and blaming them on the uppity blacks. At home with Mrs. Wheeler he could listen as she related her frustrations with a black maid. She might tell her husband again about the immorality of the blacks, how the black men don't marry black women and how they have all those dozens of kids, "breeding 'em like animals."

Later I reflected how I had gone with trembling heart to the ghetto, Harlem, fearful that a big black bogeyman might tear down the paper-thin door separating my "white" body from his lustful desires. And how it had been

a white, not a black, devil whose passions had overwhelmed him. His uncontrollable desire for blackness,
strange, mysterious, exotic—therefore stimulating and
good—simply underscores white Americans' hypocrisy.
White men created the taboos about blackness and then
fell prey to them, desiring the flesh not in spite of but
because it is black.

13 : Living as an Indian on the Navajo Reservation

*"There is really a valid reason to consider oneself as an 'other'
if one is an Indian...."*
—*Vine Deloria*, Custer Died for Your Sins

*S*ince I grew up hearing stories about Indians from my father, I always wondered what it would be like to live as an Indian. Would it be easier or more difficult to live as an Indian than as a black? To pass as a black, I had only to change myself, cosmetically. But are not Indians different from whites and blacks, psychologically, more attuned to Mother Nature? How could I enter into their world, their psyche? In 1972, I left my comfortable apartment in Washington, D.C., to live on the Navajo reservation. To get there, I boarded a TWA plane. After a couple of hours I heard the pilot saying, "There is Dodge City, Kansas." And later, "There is Santa Fe on your left." I spotted the Rio Grande, which, from its headwaters in Colorado, flows south past Santa Fe on its way to the Gulf of Mexico. Most of what I saw from the air, however, was space with no signs of people.

Landing in Albuquerque, I rented a Volkswagen and soon was on a narrow ribbon of cement in a vast desert, with a howling wind threatening to blow me and the little "bug" car into outer space. I felt diminished, as if there were nothing between me and eternity. Yet, I had thrust

myself into this vastness. I had sought to expose my loneliness, not to deny it. At Gallup, New Mexico, I turned
north. After another hour's drive, I arrived in Window
Rock, Arizona, where I checked into a small motel and
began to orient myself. I was in the capital of what is called
Navajoland, a "nation" inhabited by Indians that stretches
west from Gallup to the Colorado River and from Flagstaff
in Arizona on the south to Utah and the Four Corners on
the north. Once inside Navajoland, I was at least two hundred miles from any place I could find on my Anglo map.

The reservation, set aside by an 1868 treaty, sprawls
across twenty-five thousand square miles, about the size of
West Virginia. In this "nation" the Indians have their own
legislature, police and courts. Yet Navajos are also
American citizens, and tribal members have served in state
legislatures. With a population of one hundred fifty thousand when I went there, the Navajo tribe is the largest
Indian tribe in North America. They call themselves Dine,
meaning The People.

Driving throughout the reservation, I began to meet
native Americans. In time, through one Indian woman,
Evelyn Silentman, I came to know Bessie Yellowhair,
twenty-four, bright-eyed, enthusiastic, energetic, with a
sturdy, straight, ample body. Bessie said if I wanted to
know more about a typical Navajo family, I would be welcome to stay awhile with her family. I readily accepted the
invitation to move in with her family, who lived in a hogan,
a circular home made of mud and sticks, about forty miles
out from Tuba City, Arizona. After I moved in with the
Yellowhairs, I was one of fourteen people, eating and
sleeping in an area about the size of a bedroom in the average white family's home. The hogan had no furniture
other than one stove used for cooking as well as for heating. We all slept on the dirt floor with sheepskins beneath
and above us. And all of us slept in our clothes, for the
warmth they provided. Since there were no windows, the

inside of the hogan usually was as dark as a dungeon. When I waked each morning, I wanted to start pushing buttons to turn on some lights, to turn on some heat. But in the hogan, there was nothing to turn on—no gas, no electricity, no phones, no running water. To get water, we went by horse-drawn wagon thirty miles to the nearest windmill.

Bessie Yellowhair's father, Bahe, and her mother, Harriet, were shepherds. Indeed, the Yellowhairs, like most Navajos, built their entire way of life around sheep. They ate the meat from sheep and made clothes and their beautiful Navajo rugs from the wool. But being a shepherd in Navajoland, as I learned by taking turns guarding the sheep, is not an easy task. The sheep move about the barren soil endlessly, with one sheep needing forty acres to find sufficient grass for grazing.

Although it is not generally productive, the land is awesome in its magnitude. And the Navajos feel a holiness about their space. They deeply believe they are a part of the land, of "Mother Nature." As Bahe Yellowhair had put it, "If you take an Indian away from the land, he loses his Indianness."

I participated in several healing ceremonies, which were holistic in their approach. If you were a Navajo and became ill, you would never say, "My head hurts," or "My back hurts," or "My stomach aches." You simply say, "I feel bad all over." First you call in a hand trembler. He puts himself in a trance—one of his arms will shake uncontrollably—and he diagnoses your case, suggesting that maybe you have stepped on a snake. Or gotten too close to a tree that had been struck by lightning. This may sound atavistic or primitive to the average Anglo American, who will nod knowingly when one of his healers in a white coat says "You have cancer, and we do not know what causes it." The man in the white jacket may also say, "We'll prescribe some drugs and you will lose your hair and your appetite, and by the way, you have a year to live." In the case of the Navajo, the healing team is not dealing in time, since we are assigned to a life that ends in death, but rather in the here and now and a "wellness" that frees one from stress and pain.

If you were a Navajo, you would listen as the hand trembler prescribes a certain healing ceremony to be performed by a medicine man trained in various ceremonies. It is somewhat equivalent to a general practitioner turning you over to a surgeon or radiologist. In the case of the medicine man, he is trained to heal the mind and spirit as well as the body through medicines he prepares from natural herbs, as well as in some instances sweat baths. He is the equivalent of priest, psychologist and doctor, all in one.

Imagine for a moment you are ill and being treated. You as the patient sit in the center of the hogan, others surrounding you in a tight circle. The medicine man prays, chants and undresses you. He smears your face with paint and paints snakes on your feet. Meanwhile, a chorus of old men chant, sing, rattle gourds. This healing ceremony can go on for nine days. Learning his healing chant, a medicine man, who spends a lifetime learning his trade, will have memorized the equivalent of a Wagnerian opera. He has diligently studied, practiced, stylized his chants.

While the Navajos around me could follow the nuances, I saw and heard only the outward symbols: the dirt floor of the hogan, the drumbeat, the ongoing chants. Watching, listening, I felt mesmerized, taken back a thousand years in time.

A medicine man prays to the Holy People, the good and the evil, asking that the patient be put back in harmony with nature. The medicine man knows that he must cure the whole person, mentally, spiritually, physically. And, as I observed, the medicine man has good results in curing the sick.

Being on the reservation inspired me, later on, to do further research on holistic healing. I went to Geneva, Switzerland, to meet Dr. Paul Tournier who coined, at least for the West, the phrase "medicine of the whole person." This was what the medicine men were doing: finding and administering the right herbal or natural medications, providing a psychological ballast through support of family and loved ones, and giving the patient a sense of healing or peace of mind, peace of spirit. Dr. Tournier, author of more than a dozen books on treatment of the whole person, told me, "As much as seventy to eighty percent of our illnesses are psychosomatic."

Later, I spent time researching the work of Evarts Loomis, M.D., the first of the "medicine of the whole person" doctors in the United States. Then I went to China, accompanying a group of medical doctors and nurses. We watched eight major surgeries, such as the one shown on a 1993 Bill Moyers television documentary from China. My trip to China was in 1979, and in none of the eight major surgeries that I witnessed involving brain and heart operations, some of which lasted eight to ten hours, did the patient have any anesthesia other than one tiny acupuncture needle in one cheek. The needle somehow blocks the "message" of pain from entering the mind. Since the mind does not receive the message of pain, it can't convey this message to the body, and thus the body feels no pain. Beyond this simple explanation, the U.S. medical doctors could not put the Chinese technique into their own terminology, and they simply said it did not make sense to them. They pointed out that they had no charts, no written explanations or proof by data. It was the same on the Navajo reservation. The ancient chants, the passing of a cup of herbal tea, a medicine man painting snakes on the breasts of a patient did not make "sense." There was no data to prove that it worked.

Living among the Navajo was a more difficult experience for me than living as a black. White and black Americans basically have the same value system. Most want a better job, more money, a carpet on the floor. For the Indian, being is more important than achieving. Their goal is to be like a fish in the sea, a bird on the wing, to pass by, without leaving a trace of one's existence. The western Anglo idea has been to "conquer" nature, to disfigure a stone by carving one's name. Being an Indian is not having a certain skin color. It is not anything on the outside. It is the desire to live close to "Mother Nature," to be in harmony with the sky and earth and plants. To become an Indian, if only for a moment in time, I had to accept their value system. To "let go," as it were, of striving for materialistic goods or worldly success. To accept being in the here and now. Accepting the Indians' value system was more difficult for me than the physical discomfort of living and sleeping on dirt floors.

14: Passing as "Bessie Yellowhair"

"We must return to and understand the land we occupy."
—Vine Deloria

Bessie Yellowhair told me how her family was near starvation. She was fifteen. Her mother found an advertisement for a "live-in" maid, and the family sent Bessie to work in California. Bessie told me how difficult this had been, how she missed birds, plants, animals. City noises, dirt, smog, pollution assailed her.

Because I wanted to understand what it means for an Indian who is quiet, passive and peaceful to enter into a white society that is aggressive, loud, materialistic, I asked Bessie Yellowhair if I might borrow some of her clothes and even her name. I had stayed with the Navajo long enough that I was confident that I could pass for one of them. My hair had grown down to my waist, and I dressed the way the Navajo Indian women did, in a long fluted skirt and velvet overblouse. I scanned a small weekly, the *Navajo Times,* and found an ad:

"WANTED: loving Navajo babysitter for three children, six, four and two." The salary was twenty-five dollars a week. There was a name, Mrs. Morton, and a California telephone number. I called, and after I assured her that I could speak English and knew how to use a vacuum sweeper, she said she would arrange a prepaid ticket to Los

Angeles, which I was to get from Greyhound in Holbrook, Arizona.

Preparing to leave, I put all my identification cards in an envelope and mailed them to my address in Washington, D.C. Suddenly, I felt stripped, cast into a helpless anonymity. I could no longer produce my "preferential" cards. Nor a driver's license, checkbook, wallet, address or phone book. Inside my undergarments, I sewed a five dollar bill and a few coins. Adrift and rudderless, I was besieged with a nagging doubt: suppose I can't make it out there? What if I have made an irrevocable judgment and am permanently saddled with it? I sought solace from Thoreau, who said, "Not till we have lost do we begin to understand ourselves." Once fully committed, I felt a gradual sense of calm, of letting go.

It was six in the morning, and I, newly self-christened Bessie Yellowhair, walked away from the reservation toward Highway 264 that leads to Tuba City. I was wearing a long fluted calico skirt with a dark maroon velveteen shirt. My hair, in two pigtails, was partially covered by a kerchief tied securely around my head. Soon I found myself standing on a highway, a small flowered canvas suitcase near my feet, raising a hand, motioning for a ride. I felt the whoosh of an occasional vehicle and wondered why I had never realized the speed of an automobile until now, on an isolated highway where they zipped past with such velocity.

Suddenly a pickup truck pulled off the road, kicking pebbles into my face. Lifting my skirt, I ran toward the vehicle, carrying the flowered suitcase, and climbed into the front seat beside a man with an old, tarnished look to his skin. Distressed to realize that he was not like me, not a Navajo, I did not trust him. My adjustment was already taking hold. His assumption of superiority, and with it an unmistakable disdain, diminished my morale. I pushed myself against the door, fearing his intention.

Eventually, he spoke: "Where you heading?"

"Holbrook," I replied. I wanted to say more, but my voice gave way to a fear of betrayal. My will seemed suddenly eroded, and instinctively I threw up my guard against a vaguely felt threat. My voice came in slow motion and seemed altogether detached from the person I had been before.

"When we get there," he said in a casual but husky tone, "you can spend the night with me."

"No, no," I said, barely finding a voice in my state of shock that came not only at hearing his words but recognizing that I was almost defenseless. His truck was going seventy miles an hour, and no other vehicles were in sight. His matter-of-factness was demoralizing, and I had to assert my resentment lest I encourage and embolden him. I pondered what Bessie Yellowhair might do in this same situation. Then I heard myself saying, "You stop this car! You let me out!" My voice was not as strong or as fierce as I wished. But he did not argue. He insulted me further with a snicker, as if he was merely following his whims by obeying my instructions. He pulled off the road and without either of us saying another word, I scrambled out.

Standing alone again, the pickups and cars whizzing by, I tried to understand why I was so shaken by the man's advances. I reminded myself that I always traveled alone. But in the past I always had me, a known identity. Until now, I had not changed my name. In Indian gear, passing as Bessie Yellowhair, who was I? I was not the same person, and yet I had also separated myself from the closeness of a Navajo family. I felt my aloneness more chilling than a cold wind.

Two hours passed. I still had one hundred miles to go. Again, I heard a pickup braking for a stop. Running, climbing into a seat, I saw that the driver was a young Anglo woman wearing tight pants and a loose shirt. She had a short, mannish haircut. Newspapers and magazines were beside her, and her radio was tuned to the morning news in English.

I stared at two emblems: a statue of Christ glued to the dashboard and a United States flag decal plastered on the windshield. I reflect on the irony of our roles. She, a good, red-blooded, flag-waving Christian American, wished to communicate, asking me if I had a family in Holbrook. I felt a surging melancholia and sat silent, like a wooden Indian. In my silence I wanted to tell her: "Do not try to be kind to me, you have done all that you can do by offering this ride. As to the rest, leave me alone."

We passed Ganado and the Project Hope hospital and continued on to Steamboat Canyon. At the intersection of Highways 264 and 77, our directions parted, and after she pulled off the road to a stop, I got out. Again, I was left standing by the highway that leads due south to Holbrook. It was noon. I had for sustenance a couple of apples, and I munched on one while looking ahead to one of the loneliest highways surrounded by empty land that the eye can see. The land I hoped to travel before nightfall stretched out interminably. I felt dwarfed by this space, an inconsequential transient. God in His Heaven probably couldn't have found me in such a void.

Eventually another pickup truck braked to a stop. Running to claim a ride, I saw that the cab was filled with six adult Navajos, while the back open section held a dozen children. I climbed in with the children and we took off. Eventually, we pulled into Holbrook. The driver of the pickup stopped at a main intersection of the town, and I jumped off, waving good-bye. Then I walked to the bus station. As I entered the station, I was accosted by a drunken Indian who propositioned me for the night. As many men have seen any woman alone on the road, he saw me as a handy pickup, a usable commodity. I walked around him and found a ticket window, noting a white man, about fifty, behind a glass enclosure.

He appeared harassed, preoccupied and looked at me without interest.

Did he have a ticket, I inquired, for Bessie Yellowhair? A prepaid ticket? Without hesitation, he turned to a stack of envelopes and, flipping through them casually, came to one marked, "Betsy Yellow." He marked in his ledger "no identification," and without speaking a word, handed me the ticket. I wondered if any of the poor Indian women who accepted prepaid tickets to white households ever carried identification papers. In any case, I had passed for a Navajo, with no proof other than my appearance. Standing, waiting — the westbound bus was late — I fingered a bracelet Bessie Yellowhair had given me. I visualized her, a fifteen-year-old girl, leaving her family and the reservation. I imagined her in this same place, waiting for a bus. If she could do it, so could I.

After boarding a bus, I rode day and night, eventually reaching Los Angeles, where Mrs. Morton, accompanied by two of her children, greeted me. We walked a short distance to her car. She placed six-year-old Sandra up front with her, and I sat in the back with Jeffie, four, who stared at me incredulously. "He's curious about you," the mother said. "I told him a real 'red' Indian would be caring for him."

We arrived at an expensive, split-level home, and Mrs. Morton led me to a bedroom where I would sleep with the youngest child, Dave, age two. The next day Mrs. Morton, who had misunderstood the name Bessie Yellowhair and called me "Betsy," invited neighbors in to see a "real live Indian." They stared at me as if I was from another planet. But no one conjured up any meaningful question about Indian life. The women talked among themselves. It was clear they had no idea where I came from. Eventually, to indicate interest in Navajoland, one asked, "Betsy, how is the weather out there?"

From the beginning, Mrs. Morton gave me one clear

injunction: "The children are never allowed in the master bedroom." On the reservation, I had seen almost a complete absence of furniture and material possessions, but I noted an abundance of love. In the large Morton home, I saw an abundance of furniture and possessions and an absence of love.

One day I was making hot chocolate for the children when Morton entered the kitchen. He was watching my every move, and I spilled part of the chocolate on the stove. "That's dumb," he told me. "You are really dumb." I felt that I was. How quickly I had become that person the Mortons perceived me to be.

One Saturday afternoon, the Mortons were invited to a neighbor's home for cocktails. Before leaving, Mrs. Morton, taking the broiler from the oven, told me to "scrub that clean"; she left it in the sink. I attacked it vigorously. When I remembered the children, I found Dave and Sandra. But where was Jeffie? I again heard the mother's warning: "If anything happens to the children, you are responsible!"

I ran to the playground but he wasn't there. A bit frantic, I hastened to a neighbor's. No Jeffie. And then out into the streets, where cars moved, strangely impersonal, in and out of the driveways. Panic mounted. My eyes fastened on car bumper stickers, as if they might provide a clue to his whereabouts: "I'm the Greatest" and "Down with Hot Pants!" Then from behind one of the long parked cars, Jeffie appeared, riding calmly along on his bicycle. I ran to him but did not scold him. I took him in my arms, and, astonishingly, found I was crying.

We returned home just moments before the Mortons entered. He went to his stereo, and she walked to the oven, without asking about the children, and removed the broiler. Taking it to a bright light, she inspected my cleaning job. I watched her drop the broiler in the sink, demanding, "Do this over!"

Almost mindlessly, I scrubbed the broiler, recalling Bessie Yellowhair's account of a similar episode and how she had cried herself to sleep "because nobody had ever talked to me like that before." I remembered her story of having ironed shirts all day only to have her employer tell her harshly, "Do these over!" As Bessie knew, it was not the work that kills you but the deliberate effort to bruise your spirit, to nullify your humanness.

That night, too exhausted to sleep, I lay on my cot wondering if I was whole and human. The thought of escape floated around me, like an apparition, but my will had been sapped. I had transformed myself into a helpless "Betsy" so completely that I felt enslaved, trapped, incapable of action. In the eyes of the Mortons and all their neighbors, I was Betsy, a dumb Indian from a reservation with little or no culture as they envisioned culture to be.

I had momentarily lost my grip, forgotten who I ever was. But like a hungry animal on the prowl, I instinctively clung to the certainty that salvage was possible. I had worked my mind into a melodramatic state and was persuaded that my way of life depended upon my getting out of that cot. Yet, the thought of doing something of which the Mortons would disapprove almost immobilized me.

My body moved. Once off the cot, I quickly slipped into Bessie Yellowhair's skirt and overblouse. I pulled on a pair of white socks and the tennis shoes Navajo women generally wear. I tied an old kerchief tightly around my head. I walked down the steps, cautious but determined. I did not know the hour, but it was still well before dawn. All was quiet, except for the pounding of my heart. A sense of guilt troubled me. As the steps creaked under my weight, I was relieved to see the door to the master bedroom was shut.

Stumbling through the darkened den-kitchen, I reached an area where I knew there were sliding glass doors opening onto the patio. Before retiring, Mrs. Morton had drawn heavy damask drapes across the glass, and I fumbled through the folds, searching for the lock. My hands trembled as I located the lock, but I couldn't work it open. "Dumb Betsy!" Morton would gloat.

After some moments I gave up. I considered returning to my room. And stay there forever? The idea reinforced my resolve. I moved as noiselessly as possible to the front door. It was a heavy, wooden door that creaked loudly when opened or closed. I clutched the door knob, and at my bidding it turned! I tried to mute the moan of the opening door. No time to be timid now, though I held my breath as I stepped into the night air, attempting to close the door without waking the family. Every sound was magnified to my ears, and I had to rein in my imagination. Would Morton, hearing his front door close, come lunging down the stairs, gun in hand, shouting, perhaps shooting?

Once out the door, I started to run, but as I rounded the house to go through the patio to the street, I collided with a cement pot for outdoor plants, and fell forward, breaking my plunge with my arms. "Dumb Betsy" again! I rose quickly and headed for the street, walking rapidly and resolutely.

I walked for what seemed like miles. Passing under street lights I saw row after row of curried lawns and tidy development houses in barricaded security. I longed to see the lights of an automobile. When at length, lights appeared, I suddenly was fearful it was the police. Frantically, I dashed into a cluster of bushes, tearing my clothes. Exhausted and frightened, I threw myself in the dirt. Had Morton discovered I had fled and called the police? I listened intently, half-expecting to hear a siren. What would I tell the police?

When all was quiet again, I emerged from the shrubbery and resumed walking at a fast pace. In the distance, there was an expressway off to my right but a deep gully and a high fence prevented my crossing over to it. Finally I reached a service station but it was closed. Nearby, however, there was an outdoor telephone booth. After nervously checking the directory for taxi companies, I memorized the number of one and ripped open the center portion of my brassiere, into which I had sewn some bills as well as small coins. I inserted the coin, dialed the number and, getting a response, said I wanted a cab. The voice at the other end seemed impatient. "Where are you?"

In an area called University Park, I said. I rushed to explain that I was using a telephone at a service station. "It is a Standard station."

"I don't have time for games," the voice replied and the line went dead.

Why, I chastised myself, hadn't I learned more about my location? I started walking again and near a darkened store I spotted a delivery truck. It was parked and on one side it had large lettering, *The Los Angeles Times.* A young man was hoisting papers from the back of the truck and stacking them at a front door of an unlighted building. As I came closer, I noted he had a beard and hair to his shoulders, was wearing faded well-worn denims and from all appearances might be classified as a hippie. I moved into his orbit slowly, trying not to arouse suspicion. The impersonal, cold environment of brick and mortar surrounded us, the darkened buildings standing in eerie gloom.

"Where," I asked, "are all the people around here?"

"I hate this area this time of the morning," he replied, showing no particular interest in me as he continued stacking his papers.

"Those bundles look heavy," I said, trying desperately to be casual, not to betray my anxiety.

"Each one weighs six pounds."

I was capable of only wooden thoughts, so I stood silently watching him. Once he had finished piling the papers and started back to his truck, I asked if I might ride with him to a taxi stand or a bus station. I feared that he might balk because my dress was badly torn and stained with blood from my fall in the Morton patio. He looked at me without judgment. "I'll have to deliver my papers first."

I climbed up into the cab beside him. We started out and after a silence, he asked, "Where you coming from?"

The Navajo reservation, I told him. In Arizona.

After some miles and another silent inspection of my bloodied torn clothes, he eventually asked, "Did someone just put you out on the highway?"

Something like that, I responded.

"But that's terrible!"

I told him I had asked for it, in a way.

"I know where there's a police station," he said, eyeing me keenly. "I can take you there."

"I don't mind going to the police," I said, hoping he would not think I was a fugitive, "but I would rather not." At this point, I knew I must do whatever he determined. After he made a half-dozen stops to leave papers at luxurious food shops and drugstores, I saw new housing developments spread back to the Santa Ana Mountains. We passed the impressive new University of California in Irvine and I noted a modern, sprawling Fashion Island shopping center and a medical plaza and again more rows of expensive homes. "I can drop you at the bus depot in Newport Beach," he told me. And there he waved good-bye. The station was closed, but a sign on a door informed me that the first bus to Los Angeles would depart at six in the morning. I calculated I must have escaped the house about three hours earlier. Yet, had I really escaped? I could not shake the idea that I was a fugitive until I got far beyond the reach of the Mortons.

In the small pocket where I had sewed some money I had a couple of telephone numbers, including the number for my employer. In spite of my better counsel I found myself standing in a street phone booth, dialing the Morton number. After four rings, a very sleepy Mrs. Morton picked up. By her dull "Hullo" I knew they did not hear me leave.

I told her briefly that I did not want them to waken and find me gone, without some explanation. Her silence was almost wrathful. Turning to her husband, she said, "It's — it's Betsy." Then in a tone of contempt, "She's run off."

After convincing me I was disloyal, ungrateful, traitorous, she changed to a voice of sweet reasonableness. "Betsy, what's wrong? What are you doing—away from home!"

I was going back to the reservation, I told her.

"But why, Betsy, why? What happened?"

It was all too different, I said.

"Why different?" Her voice skirted the edge of hysteria.

I stood mutely, unable to answer.

"Betsy," she screamed into the phone, "how is it different?"

I could not think of any explanation, and my silence infuriated her. She slammed the phone down, leaving me aching with new fears.

Now surely they would call the police. They at once would check their fine silver, their jewels. If they should imagine anything missing, Betsy would be accused.

In agony, I waited for the bus, stationing myself in an alley, to avoid the police, the Mortons, anyone seeking to block my increasingly desperate passage. When I saw the bus approaching, I ran, almost as if I were fleeing to an air-raid shelter. The bus would be a haven from the threatening past. The bus made several stops, but I stayed aboard with the last lap of my journey as slow as eternity.

In the Los Angeles terminal ladies' room, where once the real Bessie Yellowhair had spent a night on a hard bench, I splashed cold water onto my face. Then I retrieved from my undergarment the home number of a lifelong friend, Jo Elliott. Yes, of course, said Jo, answering my call. "You are always welcome!" Then she asked, "Where have you been? What's up?" I said it would take awhile to explain. Jo was leaving almost immediately on an overseas trip. Alone, back in the Anglo world, I had the quiet and space and time to sort out my separate selves. For awhile, I asked: who actually am I? In this period of coming back to my other self, I realized the strength of character required to assert your own personality when others see you as dumb, lesser than themselves. I had truly started to believe that the Mortons had a right to shape my mind, my perception of myself. In solitude, I came to understand how one could easily fall prey to a domineering spouse or lover or group so that escape—back to the real self—becomes nearly impossible.

15: Living as a Wetback — Swimming the Rio Grande

"You put a million men along this border. It won't stop them from coming across."
— *W. G. Luckey, border patrolman*

"There are a million people coming over," border patrolman W.G. (Bill) Luckey told me, as I rode in a van with him along the U.S.-Mexico border. "And they have a million ways to cross."

I did not tell Luckey, but I too wanted to be one of those million, to attempt to cross without documents, as did the wetbacks. And why was this seed planted within me as what I wanted most in life to do? A desire rising no doubt from questions. Once the land I was traversing with Bill Luckey belonged to Mexico, and then Americans took it and it became our land. And at times Americans sent representatives to Mexico and urged Mexicans to come here and work. Now I watched border patrolmen such as Luckey apprehend, handcuff and jail the Mexicans. I was a part of the history of U.S.-Mexican relations. If I better understood this history, would I not better understand myself?

I had heard about "the olden days" from my father.

"When I was growing up, the United States did not have illegal aliens," he once told me. He reminded me that

153

most early immigrants, as our own forebears, came from Europe, and the gates were so open that almost anyone with steamship fare could make it here. The Statue of Liberty welcomed the tired, the poor, the huddled masses yearning to be free. My ancestors, the Europeans and especially Anglo-Saxons, were warmly received as legal immigrants. President Kennedy summed up this experience for all Americans when he said, "We are a nation of immigrants."

Now we live in a different era from my father's time. The United States, like most other countries, has quotas. Authorities require documents. But those without documents cross in record numbers, no one ever being able to give a definite figure of how many illegals there are in the United States. Estimates vary from two to twenty million.

In Washington, D.C., before leaving for the U.S.-Mexico border, I got acquainted with Raúl Yzaguirre, head of the National Council of La Raza, an organization working for Hispanic rights. I arranged to stay awhile in the home of his sister, Teresa Tijerina, in the Texas border town of McAllen.

One day, leaving all my personal possessions in Teresa's home, I boarded a bus crowded with Mexicans. I carried no identification papers whatsoever, but I knew that entering Mexico would be the easy part. The bus rolled up to the port of entry and guards waved us through. Immediately we were in Mexico, in a town called Reynosa, where I stepped off the bus, without passport, Social Security card, traveler's checks, Visa or American Express, only some bills and a little change in my pocket. I was dressed simply in old slacks and a blouse. I had told Teresa that I would be gone for awhile and would return for my personal belongings, but she had no idea of my whereabouts. I notified no one in the United States where I was or what I was doing. Moreover, I knew no one in the

Mexican town. I stood for a moment, lonely, reduced in spirit to a being smaller than a grain of sand.

I walked to a park, and, sitting on a bench, I overheard two men talking in Spanish, a language that, over many years, I have come to understand. They were planning a crossing. One said he wasn't well, he couldn't go. I concentrated on the other. He was about five-foot-eight, in his mid-twenties, with a serious face, Indian features, with aquiline nose, high cheekbones and abundant, straight black hair. Instinctively, I felt I could trust him with my life. I was aware that it often is the stranger who proves to be my brother, my friend.

The other man was leaving when I approached. Nodding toward the nearby Rio Grande River, I asked in Spanish, "Is it difficult?"

"You want to cross?"

"Yes."

"To get a job or something?"

"Something," I said. I dropped my head in silence. Perhaps my silence and bowed head led him to believe I had committed a serious crime and must escape quickly.

"Your past," he said, "is not important." He was a simple man who saw me as he saw himself, a vulnerable, defenseless person. He accepted me as the poor of this world always seem to accept one another, at face value. Just as he knew he would be classified as "criminal" for swimming the river, he saw me as one who, like himself, could not qualify for documents for one of a thousand reasons.

"If you don't have papers," he almost whispered, "that is your business."

We began to move out of the plaza, unconsciously assuming a conspiratorial tone. "Another person drowned yesterday," he said in a low voice. I nodded, having seen a one-paragraph item in the McAllen newspaper about the drowning of another wetback attempting to cross.

We walked north, two persons among a milling throng, coming to know one another, curious about our dreams. I learned his name was Cesar Guerrero Paz, and he was born in a remote village in the state of Michoacan. Guerrero was eighteen when his father died, and his mother looked to him, the eldest of her eight children, to become head of the family. Guerrero headed north. He hitched rides on trucks to Reynosa, went to the Central Plaza where we had met, and encountered two other youths. They swam the river together, then parted. Guerrero worked at various jobs for a year, never being detected and sending home most of what he earned. But after a year, hearing through a friend that his mother was ill, he went home to see her. He was with her for two weeks. "And then she died." When we met he was again en route to *el norte*. His two younger brothers worked in the fields in Mexico, and he was the sole support for his four sisters. He spoke fondly of his sisters, relating their names and ages.

"Help me," I pleaded, "as you would a sister." I knew he planned to cross, and I wanted to go with him.

He warned I might be attacked by snakes, wild animals, or my flesh torn to shreds by thorny cactus and brush. "Everything you touch scratches, tears, bites or is poisonous." We could also encounter armed agents of *la migra*, the Immigration and Naturalization Service. "They are all along the river. They have seeing devices. They talk to each other on radios. And they have aircraft overhead." He spoke as though we were two small people going against an army of trained men with the world's most sophisticated weapons. And we were. Besides *la migra*, we would face rifle-carrying Texas farmers and ranchers, city policemen and sheriffs and their deputies, as well as armed vigilantes who often with impunity shoot a wetback and throw him into the river.

La mujer, a woman, Guerrero said, is especially vulnerable. "There are men all along the river who assault and rape the women they catch coming in." He waited for me to say I'd changed my mind. He took my silence to mean I still wanted to cross. Then he said it was the same with him. He had no choice.

"I think we could use an inner tube and swim across with less splashing," he reasoned, warning that "too much splashing is like waving to *la migra*." I walked with him to several homes in a nearby neighborhood or barrio. He eventually found an inner tube which was no more than a collection of patches held together by a bit of rubber. It would not hold air.

"It's late," Guerrero said, and I was surprised to learn it was after nine in the evening now and very dark. Guerrero advised against crossing this late. Since he had assumed the role of a "brother," I acquiesced. Tomorrow, he suggested, in the evening, we could meet, and he pointed to a particular sagebrush. "Six-thirty is a good time, about dusk." He added it would be a time when visibility would be the poorest, "before *la migra* can effectively use their night-seeing telescopes and track us down." We parted, and I found a small hotel. I was without any luggage, but the clerk asked no questions.

The next evening, I walked toward the river and along the levee. Would Guerrero keep the appointment? Then, I wondered, why should he? What would be in it for him? Yet, I trusted him. Somehow I felt certain I had appealed to his highest sense of honor, his respect for his sisters. I strained my eyes for the meeting place. Then, half hidden behind a sagebrush, Guerrero's face appeared.

He greeted me with a nod. I reached to touch his hand to convey my pleasure in his presence. Guerrero said he had again sought but not found a suitable inner tube we might use. "We will cross without it." Again he reminded me not to splash while swimming.

We walked to the river. I knew that I might lose my life, and this possibility created a heightened awareness of the beauty of this earth. Was this what is meant—that one must be willing to give up life to find it? Facing difficulties, I felt enriched, and sharing these dangers with Guerrero, I took on some of his courage. I felt an overflowing sense of gratitude that he had allowed me into his world.

At the riverbank, he removed shoes, trousers. Water that previously had appeared muddy now glistened. I saw a million silvery coins dancing on its surface.

I took off my shoes, slacks and blouse and placed them in a plastic bag, which Guerrero had provided. I was down to shorts and halter.

Guerrero took the plastic bags with our clothes and without hesitation waded into the Rio Grande. I followed. I imagined border patrolmen on the Texas shore, their binoculars trained on us.

We stood ankle-deep in the water, and Guerrero, noting that my body was shaking, reminded me that in crossing it is not so important to be a good swimmer but to have con- fidence, to be sure of yourself. "Many drown," he said. I had read that often swimmers panic when they meet an unexpected swift current or treacherous eddy.

The water beat with whirlpool force about my knees. Then I was waist-deep. I felt my feet sweep off the sand. I began to swim, splashing noisily, slapping legs and arms against the water to keep up, the way I learned in Texas creeks. In my near panic, I was not swimming but franti- cally stirring up the waters. I saw Guerrero propelling him- self forward with strong, silent strokes. He shortened his distance and swam beside me. *"Estoy aquí,* I am here," he reminded me. My legs and arms grew less tense, I began to control my breathing. His reassuring words provided me additional strength. I lengthened my strokes, making every motion surer, smoother, swifter. Once, I tried to look at the shore to see if armed guards were waiting to arrest us. As I searched for *la migra,* I forgot my breath- ing. Water gushed into my mouth, and I coughed loudly.

"Silence!" Guerrero reminded me. I attempted to banish *la migra* and armed vigilantes from my mind. Again concentrating on my breathing, I regained confidence, knowing that Guerrero was swimming beside me.

We reached the shoreline and waded into the Promised Land.

Guerrero handed me my plastic bag, and each of us disappeared into the brush. After removing our wet clothes and getting into dry ones, we climbed a steep embankment. Silently, we paused for breath trying to prepare ourselves against a sudden attack. All was jungle quiet. We came to a clearing.

"Listen!" Guerrero whispered. Hearing the drone of a plane, we both fell to the ground like soldiers under an attack.

"Here, hide!" Guerrero commanded, pulling me after him into a shelter of thorny bushes. I was scratched and bleeding, but fear blocked any noticeable pain. We barely breathed, listening to the plane overhead.

Like any "fugitive," I did not want to find myself behind bars, denied the right to see the sky, reduced to a numbered object, easily lost in a maze of statistics, my whereabouts a mystery to family and friends. We stayed motionless in the bushes. When we heard the drone of the plane diminish, we each breathed with relief. Psychologically we had crossed the "greatest of all rivers." To the wetback, the Rio Grande is like Dante's allegorical River Styx—it separates the hell of poverty and starvation from Heaven-on-Earth, a job, food, money for one's family.

But even in the Paradise, Guerrero, as an illegal, would forever be halfway in hell. I thought of his future life. He would always have to hide, a fugitive from justice, subject to every abuse as a wetback. Blacks and Indians might be second-class citizens, but he must find work without even that rating.

In the moments when I have cast my lot with others less

fortunate, I have felt myself singularly blessed. Why is there always an escape hatch for me? Why was I born so lucky? I tried to imagine the loneliness Guerrero would suffer in a land whose cultural and social values are foreign to him. He spoke only a few words of English, he was hundreds of miles from his loved ones. Guerrero could not write to his family, and they could not write to him, for they did not know how. Yet he, like millions of others, would have to make it when odds were stacked against him. "Don't move—*no te mueves,*" Guerrero said, suggesting we remain hidden in the bushes for half an hour. If we triggered sensor devices in *la migra* headquarters in McAllen, agents in scout cars would be speeding to an area a fast-moving wetback would reach after thirty minutes' travel. But by remaining hidden we would not be in that area. "They'll think a jackrabbit has triggered the sensor, and they'll leave," Guerrero explained.

"How," I asked Guerrero, "do you know so much about *la migra* and their sophisticated weapons?"

"We talk endlessly in the Reynosa plaza and in our villages about them, how they operate. Our lives depend on our knowing."

What would he do now, I asked. Did he think he could find work?

"There's plenty of work in this country," he said. "I will take any work. On my first trip, I mopped floors, mowed grass, worked in a packing plant, ran an elevator." I looked anew at his Indian face, his dark skin, and realized he was unschooled, with no special skills. Yet he told me, "My bosses have all liked my work." His last job was as a dishwasher in a Dallas restaurant. He planned to return there and, if *la migra* didn't catch him, hoped his former boss would hire him again.

We agreed that once we started walking we would go in different directions so it would be easier for us to hide. I walked toward safety and friends. But he faced an unknown future with nothing more than his courage to sustain him.

Leaving Guerrero, I heard myself heaving deep sighs of relief. I felt drained of all emotions. I was back home in the United States. Yet a part of me seemed to have walked off with Guerrero. I boarded a bus to McAllen and made my way back to the home of Teresa Tijerina.

"I crossed the Rio Grande," I told her. I admitted I could not have done it on my own, but that someone wonderful had helped me. I felt a special kinship by now with Guerrero, and this came through in my description.

"Will you," she asked, "see him again?"

"No," I said.

Yet, since that time I think I have seen his face a thousand times. Sometimes the face looks furtive. Sometimes he is serving a meal. Sometimes he is among his buddies. I see them on the streets of Washington, on the streets of Fort Worth. They are looking for jobs. They will work hard, perhaps get deported, and swim the river once again. Always, when I look into their faces, I see Cesar Guerrero, and I want to say, *"Hola! Amigo!* I know you."

16: Crossing with Nannies

"I was acting more as a mother."
—Zoe Baird, President Clinton's first choice for U.S. attorney
general, admitting to hiring an illegal immigrant

"Maybe Zoe Baird was right.... Maybe American parents have
decided that the house is best maintained by the Latino.
—Richard Rodriguez, MacNeil-Lehrer Report,
April 8, 1993

From McAllen, Texas, I traveled nearly a thousand miles westward. On an earlier trip to El Paso, I had become acquainted with some Catholic nuns, and I went to their convent, where I stayed in a private room. In my talks with the nuns, I told them my plan: to cross with undocumented workers. One nun talked about a means of doing so, *el punte negro*, a black bridge.

"It's a Southern Pacific Railway bridge used only for freight," she told me. "Mexicans run across this black bridge—there are no checkpoints—and once across the bridge, they are here in El Paso."

The next morning, I left all my identification papers with one of the sisters, boarded one bus, changed to another and, without anyone asking for documentation, arrived in the Mexican town of Juarez. Before leaving the bus, I asked the driver, "Where is *el punte negro?*" He gave directions, and I walked to the bridge.

I found sixty to seventy undocumented workers standing on the Mexican side, ready to make a dash. Looking over to the U.S. side, I saw one patrolman sitting at the wheel of a sedan. He held a small army of people at bay. Along with the others, I waited in the sun. I got acquainted with two young men, Roberto and Joaquín, both in their late twenties and somehow related. Both wore clean slacks with short-sleeved cotton shirts, open at the neck. Their hands were smooth and white, indicating they were office workers, a class apart from others around us, laborers who will dig ditches, bend and stoop over crops, pour concrete, clean abattoirs.

"We might be sitting here all day," Roberto said after a two-hour wait. We were seated on an embankment, three in a row. As we talked, two Mexican women walked along a path below, then retraced their steps and climbed up beside us on the retaining wall. Seeing us as co-conspirators, one, somewhat hesitantly, said in Spanish, "We want to cross the bridge." I moved to one side, and they sat beside me. "Have you worked for the Anglos?" one asked. She volunteered they came north from Durango, having heard there were jobs as domestics in El Paso. Without needing to dissemble, I said that I had. We discussed the price that maids earn in El Paso, and to them the wages sounded fabulous. One of them remarked, "No woman earns such money where we come from."

Taking my eyes off the black bridge, I studied the would-be domestics, neatly dressed in slacks and shirts and carrying only small purses. Neither of the women was rushing to divulge case histories. No one questioned them. They sought greater independence. But like me, they had linked their immediate future with the two men in our midst. Each hoped we would have the strength to cross the bridge together. As we waited, we saw the black bridge as our hope. Focused on our plan, we scarcely spoke. Yet we had silently agreed to trust one another. In those moments we were closer than kin.

By mid-morning, the heat had become steamy, and we feared the immigration car would remain as a barrier. So

we walked east, toward Chamizal Park, where Mrs. Jimmy
Carter and Señora Carmen Romano de López Portillo,
wives of the presidents of the United States and Mexico,
held a 1977 Good Neighbor meeting. The park takes its
name from the Chamizal Treaty that returned 630 acres
along the disputed U. S. border to Mexico.

With Roberto and Joaquín and the two women,
Carmen and Cristina, I watched the Rio Grande. Here it
was unimpressive, a sluggish small stream flowing through
a manmade canyon separating jobless workers from U. S.
factories and fields. Carmen, the older and taller of the two
women, with ample bosom and hips, tied her long, black
hair in a bun at the nape of her neck. Her dark eyes spoke
of a woman's inner life and personal sadness. Yet, she was
quick to smile and break into laughter. In Mexico, she
made candles, earning pesos that came to a dollar a day in
U.S. money.

As we strolled the embankment, I learned that Cristina,
who was petite, slender, with her black hair cropped in a
casual, modern style, was married and the mother of a two-
year-old child. But her husband, she confided, beat and tor-
tured her. At the mention of the child, tears dropped from
her eyes. *"Dura, muy dura.* Life was difficult, very difficult," she repeated, reliving a scene that had torn her heart
asunder: leaving her child with her mother she headed for
el norte to earn money for the child's support.

The five of us, having chosen Joaquín as our leader,
walked west for two hours through debris, sand, stone and
brush. Here the country of Mexico and the states of Texas
and New Mexico joined, and the Rio Grande, flowing
from the Rockies in Colorado, turned east, searching its
way to the sea at Matamoros and Brownsville. We grew
weary of the dust and heat.

Eventually, Joaquín shouted: "Here! We'll cross here."
The men turned to one side. We removed shoes and slacks,
leaving on our shirts and shorts, and stepped into the

water. My bare feet struck against slippery rocks on the river bottom. Regaining my balance, I heard Cristina give a quick cry as she sank under the water. Roberto and Joaquín grabbed her as Carmen and I fished frantically for Cristina's purse, which was floating downstream. Undoubtedly thinking of her young son, Cristina wailed loudly, then broke into uncontrolled sobbing.

Joaquín slapped her face. "Our most dangerous moments are ahead," he warned. "We must move quickly!" Forgetting the purse, we plunged ahead, reached shore and redressed quickly.

We sprinted along railway tracks, then moved in single file across a freeway, dodging the cars that bore down on us. Horns blared and brakes screeched. Had Cristina been killed? I dared not look back or to either side, nor did I focus on the cars. I used all my strength to follow Joaquín.

Adrenaline rushed through my body. No longer thinking, my body took over and fear moved me. I smelled the fear and the hatred many white Texas police and vigilantes feel for brown illegals. We dashed toward what we hoped was cover.

Carmen screamed for help, and, slowing their pace, Roberto and Joaquín grabbed her elbows and swung her along. Her feet barely touched the ground. We came to a drainage tunnel and raced into it, seeing nothing but the curved concrete walls, hearing only the echo of our feet pounding on the gravel remnants of storms long past.

At the end of the tunnel, we turned east, scrambled up a small hill and saw an orderly row of houses. At first glance, the scene appeared as Arcadia, a lost paradise somehow regained. The sun overhead indicated midday. We had dropped from one unreal existence into another. We strolled as if we belonged in this neighborhood of neat sidewalks, clean paved streets, well-manicured lawns and expensive homes with large automobiles parked in front. Yet we were shaken by the transition, moving so suddenly from a country of poverty to a nation of wealth, with abundance all around us.

"We must separate," Joaquín ordered. "We must not be seen walking together." By scattering, moving individually, we would be less suspect. The men increased their pace, then separated. I chose a different path and saw Cristina and Carmen swiftly turn a corner together. Each was sufficiently well dressed not to arouse suspicion. They were neither poor enough nor brown enough to be suspect.

They would scan want ads, talk with other Latinas. I felt certain they would find jobs.

Cristina and Carmen were typical of thousands of Latin American women who come to the U.S. to find work as nannies. "Formerly, the illegals we apprehended along the border were ninety-nine percent men," a veteran border patrolman told me. "We almost never saw a woman crossing the border." But by the seventies, that began to change and by the nineties, it had changed drastically.

In homes across the U.S. today, mothers and fathers give Latin American women full responsibility of watching over the house — while they work or enjoy themselves outside the home. Like Zoe Baird, these Americans hire illegal aliens from south of the border and skirt U.S. laws. If President Clinton had nominated Baird to any other federal position than attorney general, her hiring of illegal aliens would not have generated the same questions. But the attorney general is top boss of the INS, charged with preventing illegals from entering the U.S.

In the past many Anglos criticized Hispanics for not developing more individualism and for being too family-oriented. Now, U.S. mothers and fathers turn to them precisely because of that trait.

17: Smuggled to the Promised Land

"To that composite American identity of the future, Spanish character will supply some of the most needed parts. No stock shows a grander historic retrospect — grander in religiousness and loyalty, or for patriotism, courage, decorum, gravity and honor."
— Walt Whitman

Before crossing the border with illegals, I spent a year talking to Mexicans who had documents and those who did not. I spent time in Tijuana, Mexico, across the border from San Diego, with migrant Mexican farm workers such as Lola Barragán and Pascual Jimez Martínez, both in their early forties and with documents entitling them to work in the U.S. I stayed awhile first in the home of Lola and her family and later in the home of Pascual and his family. Members of their extended families had built the houses, which were frame, cracker-box style with indoor plumbing and electricity. I got up when their alarms sounded at quarter to five in the morning, and I rode with them across the border and worked with them picking tomatoes in a California field owned by Robert Richardson.

After swimming the river from Reynosa to McAllen and crossing from Juárez into El Paso, I returned to Tijuana and to the homes of Lola Barragán and Pascual Jimez Martínez. "Do you want to join us again, picking tomatoes?" Jimez asked.

"No, not this time," I told him. "I want you to help me meet a smuggler." I heard a lot about smuggling from the border patrolmen, who indicated that probably half of the illegals entering the United States are smuggled in. "The smuggling of aliens is a large-scale, highly organized operation," a patrolman told me. "We catch only the small fry. The big ones always get away." While in the Martínez home, I met Beto Sánchez, who knew a great deal about Mexicans being smuggled across the border. Sánchez helped me meet and talk with a smuggler, his cousin, Eduardo Burriaga.

While Sánchez was a Mexican citizen, Burriaga was a citizen of the U.S. He had dark, flashing eyes, dark skin, straight black hair, a soft voice that cradled words lyrically. After Sánchez introduced us, he left, and Burriaga and I sat over cups of coffee. Did he feel more gringo, I asked, or more Mexican?

"I am Mexican. I came to that. But it was a long process. As a child, I was taken back and forth across the border. My mother died, my father remarried. I never thought he wanted me around. I lived in the streets, robbed and stole. I was sent to a U.S. reform school. Then I decided to join the U.S. Army. And I was sent to Vietnam. There were scores over there like me. We Chicanos died like flies, more than the white boys. I didn't like shooting the Vietnamese peasants. I thought I was more like them than the Anglos who sent me there. This thought blew my mind. War will get you, one way or another. And I ended up in a mental ward, at an army hospital near Washington, D.C. I did not know who I was. On my release, I returned here to Tijuana to be among my people."

In me, Burriaga found a listener. He seemed to like telling his stories to one who was interested, yet nonjudgmental.

With Burriaga, I walked the streets of Tijuana, the

largest of Mexico's border cities, looking into narrow, dark corridors and mysterious, cramped, shrouded shops, all emitting strange odors, sometimes sensuous, often foul. The raucousness of voices and traffic noises, the overpowering smells and congestion reminded me of other exotic, nefarious cities, where millions live precariously, each moment knowing they were never promised a tomorrow. "Here in Tijuana," Burriaga said, "you can find anything, any kind of male or female prostitution, any contraband, any kind of deal or dope, cocaine, heroin, any kind of gun for hire."

In order to talk to Burriaga, I often stood in the lobby of the Carlos Primero Hotel, where he worked as a desk clerk. I watched as he accepted Mexican pesos equivalent to two dollars from a short, thin Mexican with an overly fat woman companion. He gave the man a key and the couple walked up a flight of stairs. Burriaga was bored by this job but became animated when he talked about his war years and his experiences as a guide or, in Mexican, *coyote*, smuggling aliens across the border.

His tales of a one-man enterprise reminded me of conversations with border patrolmen about a highly organized smuggling operation. Yet the Burriagas must be multiplied by the thousands. *Coyotes* are like prostitutes: for every one who is part of a highly organized ring, there are a thousand or more who are individual entrepreneurs.

Burriaga explained that "tubes" or drainage ditches link Tijuana and San Diego because the two cities once were one, and they continue to share the same water sources. Bandits and murderers now use the tubes as hideouts, and illegal aliens cross through them from Tijuana into the suburbs of San Diego. One day Burriaga showed me a tube three feet in height that he had crawled through smuggling a Mexican illegal to the U.S. "You are on your hands and knees and you fear you'll never get out," he remembered. "It's darker than hell. You can't see, you can't hear, you can only smell. The stench is overpowering. We covered our noses with handkerchiefs. Even so the smell is so overpowering you can hardly move."

Like many men, Burriaga would rather talk about his life to a woman who will listen than engage in any of the so-called manly or sexual pursuits. He never questioned my need to understand his work or asked whether I was documented or undocumented. But he knew tens of thousands of people in Tijuana wanted to cross into the U.S. and did not have papers. For him, I was one of them. One day I overheard Burriaga tell a friend of plans to smuggle a small group through one of the tubes, and I asked if I could cross with them.

"Oh, I'd never take a woman through the tubes," he objected. "You couldn't stand it."

"I don't have papers," I said. "I have to try."

The next day, Burriaga and I went to a coffee shop so small it had only three booths. By prearrangement we met José, a young man in tight-fitting trousers and silky shirt. A second man, Ramón, from the interior of Mexico, a farm laborer dressed in work clothes, joined us. Both men were about thirty. Ramón knew Tijuana well, having been here several times for crossings. He usually worked in the U.S. for six months, then went back to his Mexican village. This had been his pattern for the past ten years. For his earlier crossings, "I managed on my own. But now, *la migra* makes it more difficult." So he was turning to Burriaga for help in crossing.

Heat radiated in the cafe, and José unbuttoned his silky shirt to the waist, fanning a section of it across his chest. He said he was worried about *la migra* capturing him, "taking my picture and putting me in jail." When Burriaga told him I would be crossing the border with them, José objected. "It's bad luck, to have a woman along." Burriaga paid him no mind and said we four would cross by crawling through a tube.

We agreed to leave at midnight. Shortly before departure, I stood with Burriaga, José and Ramón on a sidewalk outside the Carlos Hotel. A vagrant slept at our feet. Police sirens wailed, and, in an adjoining bar, armed officers arrested a man wanted for murder. Evil and death swirled around us, and amidst it all, innocent people stepped through the deprivation, glad to have lived another day.

We all were edgy. Noting that José actually was trembling with fear, I quietly mentioned this to Burriaga. Then he blurted out to José, "She thinks you are scared."

"I'm not scared," José protested.

"You shouldn't have told José that!" I chimed in to Burriaga.

"It's important we all know how each feels," Burriaga replied.

I told José that I didn't think he was scared, just nervous. And I added that I was nervous too. To prove my point I reached out and touched him. It was a hot night, and my hands were icy cold.

"We should not be talking so loud like this," José said. "I fear the Mexican police. If they arrest us, it will be worse than *la migra*. I know how tough they can be. They'll throw you in jail, and you can stay there forever."

The thought chilled me. I was with strangers in a foreign country, with no identification of any kind. I could not prove my name if my life depended on it. I had no relatives or known address in Mexico. My pleas would sound implausible. Mexican police would probably throw me in jail and ask questions later. Ten years later.

At midnight the four of us left the hotel and walked toward the border. Burriaga described the route we'd take, and pointed in the direction of the tube. "Don't point!" José pleaded. "You look like you're signaling *la migra*."

But Burriaga, who couldn't talk without his hands, kept pointing and said we must cross the highway two by two.

José, who had been overly anxious for hours, wanted to go first. Ramón would accompany him to the entrance of the tunnel and wait for us. Then we would all crawl through together. Traffic swirled around us as Burriaga and I watched José and Ramón walk in measured, determined steps across a busy thoroughfare called Scenic Drive that parallels the border. When they had crossed, Burriaga and I followed. We hoped to look like any pedestrians, but from a car whizzing by someone shouted, "Hey, *mojados!* Wetbacks!"

Across the highway, we quickened our pace and walked in the ditch beside Scenic Drive and a fence that separates the two countries. We were still in Mexico.

Suddenly a Mexican police car cruised in our direction, and Burriaga and I dropped face down in the ditch. We could not warn José and Ramón, who did not see the police. Two uniformed men jumped from the car and seized them. Burriaga and I remained facedown in the dirt. We barely breathed.

Gingerly I raised my head. The Mexican police were questioning Ramón and José. While being handcuffed, José dropped his head on his chest. Ironically what he feared most, arrest by Mexican police, had occurred. Apparently the police had not seen Burriaga and me.

"We'll never make it to the tube," Burriaga whispered. "They'll be watching that." I lifted my head again slightly to see the police lead José and Ramón to their sedan. "We better get out of here fast!" Burriaga said.

Like furtive animals, we crawled from the ditch and under a ten-foot Cyclone fence. In a second, without risking the tubes, we were in U.S. territory, safe from apprehension by the Mexican police. But Smugglers Canyon and the Otay Mountains, where Mexicans assault, rape, rob and murder other Mexicans, still lay ahead.

As we approached the crime-infested section of the

canyon called the River Bottom, headlights suddenly flashed on us.

"*La migra!*" Burriaga warned. "They've seen us." We started running. Keeping a fast pace, we reached a zone where Customs officials checked trucks and their cargo. Vehicles with approved cargo sat there overnight.

A large truck loomed on one side of us. Seeing it as our only hope, I told Burriaga, "Let's hide in there!"

"It's locked for sure," he said. But I clamored up a tall step, tried a door, and it miraculously opened. We threw ourselves into the cab, and Burriaga closed the door. Three police cars pulled up.

I was out of view, lying on my right side. Burriaga too was on his right side, his head on my left thigh.

My heart learned a faster beat. I listened with fear to armed men with guns, knives, walkie-talkies, scopes, helicopters, sensors, the same arsenal of weapons that I had seen as a reporter in Vietnam. This time, however, I was the enemy.

Could Burriaga defend me against the brutal tactics they would use if they found us?

"We know you're under there," one agent called out in Spanish. "You bastards, we've seen you, come on out!" They had seen us only from a distance and had mistaken me for a man. They shined huge flashlights into each of the trucks but never inside the cab. They had assumed all drivers locked the cabs of their trucks in one of the worst crime areas in the world.

"Don't move," Burriaga whispered. He meant, "Don't say a word, don't take a deep breath." I melted into the seat.

"How many of the bastards did you see?" one agent called to another. Another asked headquarters for helicopter surveillance.

"I saw four but the Tijuana police got two. Probably

robbed them and threw them across the line," a voice responded.

"Damn! They've got to be under one of these trucks," one shouted in an angry and frustrated voice. Feet tramped by, walkie-talkies squawked, car doors slammed.

I feared that at any moment the cab door would be pulled open, and a long, strong arm would hurl me to the ground. The armed men wouldn't see me as a citizen with inalienable human rights but as a brown-skinned fugitive whose future lay in their hands.

Eventually, the police cars left. I raised my head slightly and looked out the right window to a green immigration van. Men were still searching through the grass, using walkie-talkies and flashlights. A helicopter sputtered noisily overhead, hovering over the trucks, shining powerful lights. The two police cars came racing back to the scene.

"They're all coming back!" Burriaga whispered.

Burriaga and I were so ridiculously outnumbered! We were like ants being chased by a herd of elephants.

"The sonsabitches must have gone into the tube," one officer shouted.

"We'll catch them when they come out," a voice answered. He radioed other agents to watch for two wets coming out of the drainage ditch in San Ysidro, a suburb of San Diego. At last the cars left. Finally, Burriaga sat up, and I moved from my pinned-down position.

I felt drained of all blood. For the first time in an hour I realized that I was not really a fugitive in hiding. Burriaga did not waste a moment:

"Let's make our move!"

We slipped down from the truck and began running toward a busy highway, Interstate 5. Burriaga was in a fast gait, and I followed close behind, all my energies devoted to keeping up. We crossed a bridge called "Avenida Caminos" and came to a typical U.S. thoroughfare. I was startled by the change.

As we slowed to a walk, I saw the symbols of the American Way: McDonald's, Jack in the Box, Colonel Sanders' Kentucky Fried Chicken, TraveLodge, Greyhound, Shell. Even though it was past midnight, open-air cafes did a brisk business. People sat outside, drinking coffee or cold sodas, eating hamburgers, licking ice cream cones, indifferent to the world of have-nots just across a fence.

Burriaga and I had not eaten for ten hours. I felt depleted, exhausted. He must have been also. Did he want a coffee?

"No," he said. "I'm worried about José and Ramón." I didn't have to ask. I knew he intended to go back to Tijuana to learn if they were in jail.

I wanted to say, "Don't go just yet." He was a living witness for me of that other world we so recently left. He was that other me, the fugitive. I was not yet sure I was in the world of abundance. Oscar Wilde said, "Those who live more lives than one/More lives must die," and in a sense I must let die the wetback I had pretended to be.

We said goodnight. I walked a few blocks to a bus station and went to San Diego, and from there I made my way to the Catholic convent where I had left some of my possessions. It was three-thirty in the morning when I took a key from under a mat, unlocked the door and slipped into the Communities of the Holy Spirit. Quietly, I tiptoed up steps to my room. Exhausted, I tried to sleep. But I tossed helplessly.

I heard brakes outside. It's the police, looking for me! Or *la migra* coming to knock on the door. Is that the drone of a helicopter overhead? Every sound was ominous. Fear grew inside me. It would take awhile, I knew, to dispel the atmosphere of danger and to reassure my mind, body and spirit that I was really safe.

18: A Photo Album

The youngest of six children, Grace was born in 1923 and grew up dur-
ing the Depression. Her father was sixty-three and her mother thirty
when she was born.

Above. *Ruth Shanks, a native of Texas, was not quite sixteen when she married Harry H. Halsell, then forty-eight.*

Right. *Harry H. Halsell in 1882, during the years he was building herds and trailing them to northern markets.*

At sixteen, Grace represented her hometown as "Miss Lubbock" in a 1936 Stamford, Texas, rodeo. She participated in a contest for women riders who were judged for speed and control of their horses. Grace, not among the winners, was then a junior in high school and the youngest participant.

Grace as a senior in high school.

Above. *Grace wrote some of the first newspapers stories about hotel magnate Conrad Hilton. Her stories appeared in the* Fort Worth Star-Telegram *in the mid-1940s.*

Left. *Gable—and Grace. On a 1946 trip to Hollywood, when she was amusements editor for the* Fort Worth Star-Telegram, *Grace chatted with movie star Clark Gable.*

Fort Worth: Grace was the first woman to ride in a B-36.

Hong Kong: Grace interviewed Chinese who carry as much as 300 pounds on a bamboo pole. After interviewing one person, Grace asked to try carrying his load. Here she's shown with two baskets filled with tea-cakes. Other coolies with whom she talked carried wood, water and lead. The trick, she says, is in the balance.

Atop Mt. Daruma: With two Japanese students, Amaki-san and Aoki-san, Grace climbed Mt. Daruma on February 3, 1956. They ate a picnic lunch, sang songs and viewed Mt. Fuji in the distance.

Hong Kong: Grace wanted to learn how difficult it was to pull a rickshaw, so she turned the tables and put the rickshaw puller, Lau Kwei, in the back seat—to the delight of the Chinese onlookers. Kwei, fifty-seven, told Grace he had been pulling a rickshaw for over thirty years but never earned enough money to buy his own rickshaw. He had to rent one.

On a junk: In late 1950, Grace lived off the coast of China on a Chinese junk with a family of nineteen, none of whom had ever lived on land.

Washington, D.C.: With Lyndon Baines Johnson in his office.

Korea: Grace was a passenger in a U. S. Air Force plane in 1955.

On an oil rig: For two years, Grace worked as public relations director for Champlin Oil and Refining Company, with holdings from Canada to Mexico. Here she's being hoisted to the mast top of an oil-drilling rig on a remote site in Wyoming. Writing for Champlin's publication, she wanted to get a feel of the work done on rigs that tower more than 150 feet.

Above. *Grace in her Washington, D.C., apartment with Dr. Jack Kenney, who prescribed a medication which, taken in conjunction with exposure of her skin to strong sun, turned her skin black. Dr. Kenney is a light-skinned black dermatologist.*

Left. *Lima, Peru: For three years, Grace wrote a daily column, "Lima Today," for the Spanish-language newspaper* La Prensa. *Here she interviews a Peruvian farmer who grew tall cotton. Peru is noted for its fine cotton.*

Grace as Bessie Yellowhair.

Fishing from a small boat off the coast of western Mexico north of Puerto Vallarta, Grace landed this big sailfish with the rod she is holding. The fish is longer than the rod.

Grace in Mexico, her "heart's home."

Top. *Three times Grace went into Mexico, leaving all her documents behind, and crossed the border into the U. S. with illegal immigrants. She is shown with two Mexicans with whom she crossed from Juarez into El Paso.*
Above. *Ecuador: Grace, stayed with long-lived people in the southern part of the country. Gabriel Erazo, right, told her, "I am 132 years old." His daughter, Deyfilia, left, said she was eighty.*

Above. *Lebanon: Palestinians in a southern Lebanon refugee camp, Rashidieh, make the "V" for victory sign. Grace is in the center (with an injured right hand). The photo was taken in 1982, shortly before the Israeli invasion of Lebanon.*

Left. *In 1993, Grace received a Lifetime Achievement Award from the University of Pennsylvania.*

PART

War Zones

SEVEN

19: Korea, Vietnam and Bosnia

"You need not change your style."
—*A CIA recruiter, asking me to become a spy*

*L*iving in Japan in the mid-fifties, I found it an easy hop over to Korea. And for me, it cost nothing. A U.S. Air Force officer issued me "orders" to travel. This was a standard military form with my name and under "rank" he wrote "correspondent." With this form in hand, I boarded an unheated cargo plane. Bundled in GI-issued woolen gear, I sat on a narrow steel "bucket seat." On either side of me were glum uniformed men, some going to Korea for the first time, others returning after rest and recreation in Japan.

How, I asked one soldier returning to duty, did he like Korea? He stared at me, with a dejected, pained expression, then muttered, "It's a hellhole."

This was the second of the big wars that had been fought in my lifetime. Surrounded by American soldiers, I reflected on what had started the Korean conflict: President Truman, operating under an umbrella of the UN, had sent American forces to right a wrong, the wrong being a June 24, 1950, attack by the North against the South. By the time I got to Korea in 1955, the fighting had stopped, but the tensions remained, with the ever-present possibility of a new outbreak.

On a drive into Seoul, I looked at a city lying in ruins. I saw little boys urinating in a small stream where only a few feet removed women washed clothes and others drew water for drinking purposes. Not in Berlin, Rotterdam, or Cologne had I seen such devastation. Two hotels were standing, and I checked into one, the Bando. After getting settled, I arranged to travel by jeep, with driver, to various camps.

"You will get a warm welcome," a U.S. Army public relations officer told me. "All of our men are lonesome to see someone from home." At that time, American servicemen, even the highest-ranking officers, could not have their wives with them. This being the case, I was one of the few American women in Korea. In setting up interviews and in moving about the country I experienced little or no red tape from the military. The men, privates to generals, welcomed me to join their off-duty hunting expeditions, usually for pheasants. One day, a pilot asked, "Want to go for a ride in my jet?" The invitation came as easily as if he himself owned the machine. I eagerly climbed in, and, streaking across the skies of Korea, I noted how beautiful that war-torn country appeared from a vantage point of thirty thousand feet.

But eventually, Korea came to represent more than the picaresque or even more than another war. Korea became a turning point in my life. It forced me to answer, at least for myself, a pivotal question: who is a good American? This question arose after I spent time with an American general in command of U.S. forces based near the 38th Parallel, the line dividing the two enemy forces, the North and the South. I had interviewed him and snapped his picture and was ready to return by jeep to Seoul. "Stay awhile," the general insisted. "You'll better know the meaning of being 'at the 38th Parallel.'" From Alabama, he was the epitome of southern charm—polite, genteel, proper, considerate, ever solicitous of a guest's needs. I said I couldn't stay, I hadn't come prepared, I had not brought a toothbrush or pajamas.

"We have extra toothbrushes. And I will loan you a pair of my pajamas."

I accepted his offer and spent several days and nights at his headquarters. I was flattered by his attentions, his treating me as visiting royalty. I had carte blanche to interview anyone in his command. When he and I entered the officers' dining room, he, the commanding general, insisted I go first. In the evenings, we sat before a fireplace, and he talked. I kept silent for the most part; my training as a reporter was to listen, to learn. And what I learned was baffling: he had been sent there to defend South Koreans, yet he hated Koreans, a people he defined as having a "lowly status." He referred to all Asians as "these colored people" and said Koreans "are hardly off their all-fours. I've made it a court-martial offense for any American soldier under my command to be caught in a Korean home. I consider this order necessary because if my men begin seeing Korean women, some will get the idea of marrying them. What would an American do with a Korean wife, once he got her back to the States? She, being one of the colored peoples, would not fit into our society!" He was determined to eradicate any intermingling and to prevent any intermarriage. His voice, usually soft, well-modulated, became more strident:

"I tell you all of this because I am a good American, and I do not want any of these colored people returning stateside. I see to it that my men have the best of food." Indeed we ate choice sirloin steaks almost every evening. "And I tell them to serve their time and get the hell out of here!"

I took notes all during his conversation with me, and he was pleased to have me do so. I have his words on paper some four decades after he spoke them. By the nineties, the so-called "white" Americans have had generations to mingle with an ever-growing Asian population in our midst. But when the general vented his hatred for "the gooks," as he referred to Koreans, I was overwhelmed by the contradictory forces striking my mind and heart.

On my return trip to Seoul, I tried to sort out my feelings. Toward me, the general was avuncular, acting like a protector, a mentor. Not once had he reached out to touch me in any physical gesture, although, since we were often alone, this might easily have occurred. It was plain his code of honor did not include physical harassment or seduction. Yet he made full use of an old technique that often weakens a woman as an individual: he was convincing me that I could use his protection, he was lulling my brain with his chivalry. His placing me on a pedestal of respect, his use of an elaborate code of etiquette — all were subtle ways to keep my mind on hold. He would never expect a woman he had treated with such respect to disagree, even to voice an opinion. And indeed, by remaining silent, I acted as he wished. Yet all that he said became questions over which I puzzled: why did he hate "these colored people"? How did he know they were inferior to him, to those of us he termed whites? Was it only a matter of pigmentation? Increasingly I knew that, as regards "these colored people," I was not aligned on the general's side. But since I had remained silent during his racist remarks, I had yet to prove where I stood.

While in the Far East, I was forced to decide another question: should a reporter, in this instance myself, ever do a "spy" operation for the U.S. government?

I was in Japan when the question arose, but the story began when I was in Vienna, back in 1952. This was the height of the Cold War, and it was difficult, if not impossible, for most U.S. reporters to travel to Moscow. Nevertheless, while in Vienna, I decided to apply for a visa. But I got no reply for three years. Then in 1955 I got a reply. "This is to inform you," the Soviet letter said, "that your request for a visa has been granted."

Reading the letter in Tokyo, I looked at a map, noting Tokyo seemed almost to touch one city in the USSR, the port of Vladivostok. At that time, Japan did not have diplomatic relations with the Soviet Union, but I reasoned that some trade must exist. I immediately set out to visit steamship and fishing companies. I became acquainted with countless managers and clerks, all of whom seemed intrigued by my determination to find a vessel bound for Vladivostok. I visited the Japanese Red Cross. I drank endless cups of tea and found the Japanese without exception polite, indicating a sincere desire to help me. The Red Cross manager eventually called. "We have a ship bound for Vladivostok." He gave me the date. And invited me to drop by for tea.

Might I board that vessel? I asked, again seated with tea. "Yes," he agreed. But there was a catch. "Our regulations say we can carry a passenger there, but regulations also stipulate that no passenger may disembark."

Buoyed by knowing that some vessels indeed went there, I continued my search, devoting three full months to my effort. I was contacted by a Japanese newspaper offering a huge sum for stories. I pointed out I did not yet have transportation. "But we are certain you will." Meanwhile, since my efforts were generally becoming well-known, at least in some circles, I attracted the attention of a Mr. Phillips, a tall, attractive Oklahoman who was introduced to me by a woman working on a U.S. servicemen's publication. He was attentive, first inviting me for coffee, later for lunch, then dinner. One evening he escorted me to a night club called the Queen's Bee. He had a table reserved near a small dance floor, and when an orchestra began playing quite loudly, he proved himself a most unusual date.

"We know quite a bit about you," he began. Each of us thinks he or she has certain secrets, but suddenly I felt denuded, unnerved. This being an era before we relinquished our personal histories to memory chips, no one knew quite a bit about me, especially in Japan.

"Your grandmother was Josie Shanks," he announced. Few outside my family knew the name of my mother's mother. He reeled off names of childhood playmates. Then surreptitiously, somewhat near the edge of a table-cloth, he produced a card, revealing he was with the CIA.

"We want you to gather information for us after you get to Vladivostok and while on the Trans-Siberian Express," he began. "You need not change your style. Act the way you do. Be a reporter. We have watched you—you act guileless, and that's perfect. Get on the train. Take a few pictures."

I was appalled. I felt betrayed, more so than ever before in my life. Moreover, I could not reply. I was burdened with shame. I felt myself the guilty party.

"Do not mention this to anyone," he urged.

I excused myself. I went to a ladies' room, where I stared at my face. All that came to mind was: God, let this decision pass. Take it away. Mr. Phillips was right: I was indeed guileless back then. I felt a strong attachment for my country, right or wrong. I presumed it was never wrong. Devoted to the U.S.A., I wanted to serve. Yet I was also a reporter. Wasn't it Jefferson who said that between a free country and a free press, he would choose the press?

Phillips asked me to see "his people," and, perhaps curious to know who was back of him, I went to the designated offices. Americans there told me what Phillips had said: I need not change my method of operation, they would instruct me what pictures to take and what other information they would need. After that meeting, I felt worse. On my next encounter with Phillips, I said I would not do it.

I dropped all my efforts to get to Vladivostok. Later, in Hong Kong I boarded a freighter and while on a thirty-seven-day cruise to Genoa I told a friend and fellow passenger, veteran *Saturday Evening Post* writer Demaree Bess, about the incident. "The U.S. government was wrong to ask you or any reporter to do any spying for them," Bess said. "The U.S. has long said the Russians used reporters, but few Americans have been aware that our government did the same."

Some years and another war later, I got another surprise after applying for press accreditation to go to Vietnam. The year was 1965, and I was working as Washington correspondent for the *Houston Post*. From other reporters in the National Press Building, I heard that the Defense Department would give any correspondent a free ticket on a commercial airliner if he or she wished to cover the Vietnam War. Checking first with *Post* owner Oveta Culp Hobby and getting her okay, I told the Pentagon I was ready. A reply came in the form of a letter from a Pentagon public information officer. I could not go, he wrote, because I had written an article while in Europe, back in the fifties, that the top brass did not like. In response I telephoned him.

Did he mean to say they kept a file on what reporters write? And put us in "good" and "bad" categories?

"Yes, indeed," he replied. He added that they considered me a "troublemaker." I took the matter up with Congressman George Mahon of Texas, who headed a committee that made funds available to the Pentagon. He reminded the Defense Department that the Americans had a "free press." I was soon on my way.

I arrived in Vietnam before the huge buildup of U.S. forces. Once there, I began skipping the official briefings, instead visiting hospitals, where I saw rooms filled with women and children with arms and legs missing due to bombs falling on them from U.S. planes.

Most reporters in the first several years of the war stayed

close to Saigon's Caravelle Hotel and went to the briefings, jotting down what General Westmoreland and other
generals endlessly repeated: "We see the light at the end of
the tunnel." The avid pro-war writers, who were of course
popular with the Defense Department, included Keyes
Beach and Peter Lisagor of the *Chicago Daily News,*
Marguerite Higgins of the *New York Herald-Tribune,* Phil
Potter of the *Baltimore Sun* and Peter Braestrup of the
Washington Post.

Prior to my 1965 arrival, a few reporters had begun to
raise questions about the war. They were ahead of public
opinion and eventually would help to mold that opinion.
But for a long time they were alone in what they were saying. These few clear-sighted writers included David
Halberstam of *The New York Times* and Neil Sheehan and
Malcolm Browne of the wire services, as well as Richard
Dudman of the *St. Louis Post-Dispatch.* Before going to
Vietnam, I had read some of their dispatches, and all that
I saw, all that I experienced, convinced me they were right
in saying this was no war the U.S. could win. It was not
popular to say so, but I pointed out that this was no new
conflict, but one in which the U. S. had been involved
since 1951 when the Americans began aiding the French,
who controlled what then was known as Indochina. I
stated clearly that despite America's great aspirations, we
had failed in our fourteen years in Vietnam.

I never understood our purpose in Vietnam. But I
thought it right that NATO forces be sent to stop the
slaughter in the former Yugoslavia. And thought this
action should have been taken earlier on, when the Serbian
warlords first began their aggression, creating the greatest
upheaval and mass suffering since the Nazis. Over almost
half a century, I saw many changes in the Balkans. I was
still in my twenties when I first went to Yugoslavia, and
even as late as my second visit in 1985, I found it a peace-

ful, beautiful country. At that time the Christians, Muslims and Jews of Sarajevo, where one-third of the city had inter-religious marriages, wanted to live as they were living, in a multiethnic, multireligious harmony. But after the demise of the long-ruling Tito and the breakup of the former Yugoslavia, a virulent nationalism took over from commu-nism, led by Milosevic of Belgrade, an ultra nationalist. Like Hitler and his "pure" Aryans, Milosevic wanted to live among "pure" Serbs of an Orthodox Christian faith. He and his warlords began a campaign to eradicate other Yugoslavs, his main victims being the Muslims in Bosnia.

In two other visits to the war-ravaged land in 1993 and again in 1994, I visited refugee camps and interviewed dozens of Bosnian victims uprooted from their homes, the men slaughtered or put in concentration camps, their wives and daughters and sisters raped. Marta, a fifty-six-year-old Bosnian woman, said, "I was held in a concentra-tion camp with a hundred and fifty women and children. I was raped, we were all raped. I saw Serbs raping children, girls as young as six and eight years old. I could do noth-ing. If a woman objected too strenuously, they slit her throat."

I can never forget the pained look in the large, dark eyes of Nadia. She was twenty, petite, standing perhaps five-feet-five. I was accompanied by a Bosnian woman physi-cian named Amra. Nadia was seated by a window, and it was a bitter cold day. "Aren't you cold?" Amra asked. "How could I feel anything so unimportant as that?" Nadia replied. She was reliving her nightmare when Serbs assaulted her village, and she and other youths fled to the hills, the Serbs following. A Serb knocked her uncon-scious. When she awakened, she was in a room with one of her arms tied to a bedpost. She was in a rape camp. The soldiers came night and day. "Even on Christmas Day," Nadia said, "eight Serbs came, saying 'Now we cele-brate.'" All eight gang-raped Nadia that day.

In some respects, the Serbs, who in late 1995 came to peace talks instigated by the Americans, went to more sinister dimensions in their evil acts toward Bosnian Muslims than the crimes committed by Nazi Germany or communist Russia in the Second World War. The Serbs unleashed the most evil weapon against civilians since germ warfare and the atomic bomb by taking the matter of rape in war deeper into depravity. In no previous war was mass rape sanctioned and encouraged by the highest officials. The Serbs did this, making rape one of their deadly weapons of war, using it to destroy the fabric of an entire people.

It is true that political rape has a long history. In the legendary account of the founding of Rome, Romulus told his soldiers to procreate with the local women. This we know as the "rape of the Sabine women." Helen of Troy was a war trophy. So was Cleopatra. And in more recent wars, German, Japanese, American soldiers as individuals and in small groups have been guilty of rape. But for the Serbs, rape became an orchestrated, fully condoned and sanctioned weapon of war used the same as tanks and guns to destroy the dignity, spirit and lives of an entire people. Studies have revealed that the Serbs raped "more than fifty thousand women and girls," said Bosnian Vice President Ejup Ganic, who added, "Not even the communists or Hitler made a systematic, sanctioned use of women as a 'weapon of war.'"

PART

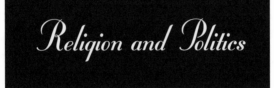

Religion and Politics

EIGHT

20: Journey to Jerusalem

"If they don't have their country, we won't have our country."
—Aviva, an Israeli Jew, speaking of the Palestinians

When I was growing up in Lubbock, I went to church and I heard the message that God had a Chosen People and a Chosen Land. I envisioned a mystical, allegorical, spiritual setting, not a place on any map. It was some decades later that I went to Jerusalem and met Bobby Brown, a third-generation American from Brooklyn, who admitted he and other newly arrived immigrants were taking land at gunpoint from Palestinians because "God gave this land to us, the Jews." I reflected that Brown could not use an Uzi to confiscate land in Brooklyn. What made it permissible for him to use a gun to take land from Palestinians? And moreover, why did American taxpayers give Israel the money to pay for the weapons to confiscate Palestinian land?

Had the Palestinians been living there for two thousand years holding the land until Bobby Brown and other immigrants could claim it? Meeting Bobby and Linda Brown and other armed immigrants, many newly arrived from the States, made a big impression on me. I had to ask myself: did I believe in a God who had a Chosen Land and a Chosen People?

In 1979, when I first went to Jerusalem, I did not know

anyone in an area Christians, Muslims and Jews generally call "the Holy Land." I began to meet women and men who represented the three great religions that came from a desert region in the Middle East. Each of these faiths is monotheistic. They hold a belief in God and they hold a belief in the same God. Because the three religions sprang from one small region, they all claim this small area as a heart center of their faith. This is true for a billion Christians, a billion Muslims and about fifteen million Jews.

Originally I planned to write about three families and three faiths. "You plan to omit politics?" one resident of the Old City of Jerusalem exclaimed. "We eat politics, morning, noon and night." The politics is all about land. Historic Palestine was small. I recall, when I was twenty and living in New York, hearing Dr. Harry Emerson Fosdick of Riverside Church telling of his early journeys in Palestine. He said you could climb a mountain "and look all over it." His journeys were before the United Nations voted to slice historic Palestine in half, giving half of the land of the Palestinians to the Jews who had been persecuted by Hitler during the Second World War. The other half was retained for the native, indigenous people, the Palestinians.

Once in the midst of Palestinians and Israelis, I experienced the reality of an ongoing conflict. I was strolling with several Palestinian women students, as well as one young man, Ghassan, on their Bir Zeit University campus near the West Bank town of Ramallah. Suddenly I saw uniformed Israeli soldiers running toward us. They were throwing tear gas, officers were shouting orders in Hebrew, and soldiers were firing rifles into the air, their shots whizzing over my head and around my ears. I turned to flee in the opposite direction, but the soldiers were all around us. Three had pinned Ghassan to the ground, and one was beating his stomach and face with the butt of a rifle. Blood was pouring from his face. Other soldiers, rushing past me, knocked me to the ground. I looked up and into the face of a soldier who in a moment of passion could have killed me.

An officer, seeing me pinned to the ground, the butt of a rifle in my face and a soldier momentarily hesitating to beat me as the others were beating Ghassan, shouted to the man over me. I saw the officer motioning to my hair and eyes, indicating I was not one of the students, that I was a foreigner. The Israeli soldier removed the butt of his rifle from my face. I scrambled to my feet, attempting to run, but my knees collapsed and I fell, not far from Ghassan. Again I saw the soldier beating him and blood pouring from his face. This was a somewhat typical day in the West Bank twelve years after the 1967 war. It was after that war that the Israelis began a military occupation of Palestinian lands including the West Bank, Gaza and East Jerusalem.

I lived constantly with the tension one feels in any war zone. To remind myself that I was in the Land of Christ, I stayed awhile with a Palestinian Christian family, who had a young daughter named Mervat. They were the Nestas family, and they lived on the outskirts of Bethlehem. Mervat, seventeen, was pleasingly plump with dark hair and dressed like so many American teenagers, in western jeans. She spoke good English as well as four other languages. The first time I saw Bethlehem, I was on a bus, with Mervat at my side. As we rode through a desert region on a hot day, I thought of all the U.S. Christmas cards with snow and reindeer. Our bus turned a corner, and I saw the little town nestled in the Judean hills. Somewhat overcome by actually viewing the town celebrated in Christian theology, I softly began to sing:

O, little town of Bethlehem
How still we see thee lie....

After hearing me through, Mervat surprised me by saying she had never heard that song. It made her town of Bethlehem seem unreal. To her, Bethlehem was not shrouded in myths but a real place where she went to school, met her friends and bought her jeans.

I spent a Christmas Eve with Mervat and her family. We built a fire outside the home and in the distance we looked to Shepherds' Field. I saw the lights of Bethlehem, flickering in the distance. Instead of turkey, the traditional Christmas fare of U.S. Christians, we roasted chunks of pork over the open fire. As we stood under the stars, eating the shishkebab, I asked Mervat's father: had his family been Christian very long?

"Yes," he said, "about two thousand years. Since the time of Christ."

And what, I asked, was the one lesson given us by Christ he felt to be most important? "Forgiveness," he said. "Being able to forgive your enemies. And start anew." The intervening years have proved how difficult forgiveness can be for both Palestinians and Israelis.

I also lived with a Palestinian Muslim family and came to know Nahla, sixteen, tall, slender, painfully shy. She was born and had lived all of her life in a refugee camp. We slept on the floor and also ate while sitting on the floor. We were seven people in one room, but across the way there were nineteen living in one room. They had no furniture. Blankets, stacked against the wall, were taken out at night for bedding. One day I accompanied Nahla to her refugee school, and I talked with the administrator, who had been educated in Buffalo, New York. He offered me a chair and sent someone for Arabic coffee. I looked about his office, which was bare, save for his desk and two chairs. With reporter's pad and pencil in hand, I asked, what did he need most?

I expected him to say books or more classrooms.

Instead he fairly shouted, "Our freedom! We need our freedom! We Palestinians must be free!" One evening,

Nahla's father, Bashir, reflected on the time when he was Nahla's age. He said it was 1948. "I was sixteen," he told me, "and living with my family when armed Jewish soldiers encircled our home, fired shots and shouted we must leave our homes or be killed." In fleeing from the soldiers, on a long march, he saw his mother die and later his father. "Now," he says, "I am a refugee in my own land." Again reflecting on 1948, he said, "They claim we Palestinians left because we wanted to leave. Why would we leave our homes? Our farms? Our animals? Our orchards? We were driven out." Bashir's family home still stands in West Jerusalem and is now occupied by an Israeli family. Even though, by the mid-nineties, peace accords had been signed by PLO leader Arafat and Israeli leader Rabin, more than two million Palestinians still were living in refugee camps.

In addition to living with Palestinian Christians and Muslims, I also stayed awhile with an Israeli family, Aviva and Reuven—she a native of England, and Reuven from New York state—on a farm between Jerusalem and Beersheba. Additionally, I stayed in many of the Jewish settlements, such as Tekoa, near Bethlehem, where I came to know several American immigrants, including Linda and Bobby Brown. "Yes, it is our land," Bobby Brown insisted. He added that he and the other newly arrived Jews staked off seven hundred fifty acres and put a strong iron fence around it. As I saw, Israeli soldiers guarded this settlement, illegal under every international law, night and day. One evening, we sat under the stars looking at the flickering lights of Palestinian villages. And Brown, with a wave of his arm, said: "All the Palestinians have to leave this land." He shifted the position of his Uzi, and repeated what he had said earlier, that God had given "all this land to us, the Jews."

After the 1981 publication of my book *Journey to Jerusalem*, I made several more trips researching U.S.

Christian support of Israel based on biblical interpretation. I concentrated on such religious right leaders as Oliver North, Pat Robertson and Jerry Falwell, who cooperate with Israeli Jewish militants on several issues, one of the most explosive being a plan to destroy the most sacred Muslim shrine of Jerusalem. To research this Christian support of Jewish militants, I signed in 1983 to go on a conducted tour of the Holy Land with Jerry Falwell. We were six hundred thirty Christians, who on arrival in Jerusalem were divided into smaller groups and sent out on buses. I was in a group that went first to the Old City, where we approached the large Muslim grounds with the imposing golden Dome of the Rock and Al-Aqsa Mosque. For Muslims all over the world, Jerusalem, after Mecca and Medina, is the third most sacred site.

"There," said our Israeli guide, pointing to the mosque, "we will build our third temple." As we left the site, I remarked to Clyde, one of the tourists, about seventy and a retired Minneapolis business executive, that the guide said a temple would be built there. But, I asked, what about the mosque?

"Oh," said Clyde, "the mosque will be destroyed. One way or another, it has to be removed. You know it's in the Bible that the temple must be built. And there's no other place for it."

Clyde was convinced that Jews, aided by Christians, should destroy the mosque, build a temple and reinstate the killing of animals in the temple, as was done in the olden days by religious Jews, all in order to please God. Many American Christians who think the same as Clyde organized a Temple Mount Foundation dedicated to raising money for Jewish terrorists whose mission is the destruction of the Muslim mosque. I talked with several American Christians who wanted the mosque destroyed, including a Baptist minister from Houston. The reverend visited me in my Washington apartment and was proud to tell me he had raised and spent tens of thousands of dollars to defend Jewish terrorists charged with assaults on the mosque. He was also pleased to relate that he had entertained in his Houston home Jewish yeshiva students, who were studying how to slaughter animals to be used as sacrifices inside the temple they planned to build.

Our group also traveled to Megiddo, located about an hour's drive north of Tel Aviv. As we left the bus, I again walked alongside Clyde. Together we looked out over the valley, and Clyde exclaimed, "At last! I am viewing the site of Armageddon." We continued to gaze at fields that in size would be lost in any Texas ranch, and Clyde talked of a two-hundred-million-man army that would invade Israel — "right here," he said. A great decisive battle would involve all the armies of the earth, and this battle, fought with nuclear weapons, would kill most of the inhabitants of this earth. I remarked that for such a big battle the valley looked very small.

"Oh, no!" Clyde said. "You can get a lot of tanks in there!"

Clyde's eyes were shining. "When this battle begins, we who are born again will be lifted up, raptured." He assured me he was not worried about the destruction of the earth, because he would not be here, but up there. Watching. With his escape hatch, he seemed actually to look forward to the destruction of Planet Earth.

A couple of years passed, and in 1985 I received a colorful brochure of a Falwell-sponsored trip. I signed on for a second tour. I was one of eight hundred fifty Christians. On our arrival we had no Christian guide to any site where Christ was born, died or had his ministry. Falwell had not arranged even one visit to a Christian church nor did he want to meet any of the Christians living there, whose forebears have remained in Palestine since the days of Christ. We had only Israeli guides, and the focus clearly was on military aspects. The Israeli guides gave us endless explanations of why the Israelis should keep all the land of historic Palestine, leaving nothing for the Palestinians.

Once, on a bus tour, I asked if we would stop in Nazareth, where Christ lived and had his ministry. "No," said the Israeli guide. He then told our tour group: we will not stop in Nazareth. No one contested the guide's decision. On the outskirts of Nazareth, however, our Israeli guide changed his mind. "We will stop in Nazareth for twenty minutes," he announced, "to use the toilet facilities." And thus we stopped. And we left Nazareth, without having seen it.

We proceeded to Jerusalem, where Falwell chose to honor Ariel Sharon, the burly general who masterminded the 1982 invasion of Lebanon. I had been to Lebanon in that year and knew Sharon had long planned an invasion to rid all of Lebanon of Palestinian fighters and Syrian troops. After saying the troops would go only twenty-four miles into Lebanon, Sharon moved them all the way into Beirut, using U.S.-made cluster bombs against civilians. President Reagan was so outraged he personally telephoned Prime Minister Begin charging that Israel was causing "needless destruction and bloodshed." The bombings were "unfathomable and senseless," Reagan said. Yet Sharon's invasion that injured or killed two hundred thousand Palestinians and Lebanese was praised by Jerry Falwell. At the banquet I attended, Falwell, introducing Sharon, said that in the annals of history, only a few great men came along. He named George Washington, Abraham Lincoln and Ariel Sharon. On another night, Falwell gave a big banquet to honor the Israeli defense minister, Moshe Arens. Before introducing him, Falwell, in an aside to Arens, said, "Mr. Minister, I want to thank you for that jet airplane you gave me." Earlier, in a visit to Falwell's home base of Lynchburg, Virginia, I had seen the jet sitting on the airport runway and been told by two Christian ministers, "It was a gift to Falwell from the Israelis."

Christians such as Falwell, adhering to a belief in Armageddon theology with Christ's return, landing from the skies north of Jerusalem, make a cult of the land of Israel. Every year, thousands of ministers go forth indoctrinated in this cult, many of them having studied at the Dallas Theological Seminary, noted for the teaching of dispensationalism. Adherents of dispensationalism, also called Armageddon theology, believe that Israel holds center stage in all the history of the world and whatever Israel does is orchestrated by God.

I went to the seminary for an interview with John Walvoord, the president, an elderly gentleman who was proud to tell me he was mentor to Hal Lindsey, whose book on Armageddon theology, *The Late Great Planet Earth,* was a best-seller in the U. S. in the seventies. Walvoord plainly told me: God gave all of Palestine to the Jews.

In living among Palestinians, I told him, I had seen their suffering. What would Christ have said and done? Would He not care about the oppressed?

"I am referring to land," he said, somewhat irritated. "You are talking about spiritual aspects." Walvoord, it seemed to me, was an example of one who makes a cult of the land of Israel and places this cult of land above Christ's teachings to care for the oppressed, to seek justice and peace.

In living my research for my earlier books among American minorities, I faced difficulties, obstacles, and, especially in the late sixties when I darkened my skin to live as a black, I discovered some people hated me for doing what I did. Controversy swept around me, but nothing in all my previous experiences equalled the backlash I received when I spoke of the plight of Palestinians. Because of an almost total sympathy for the Jews who had suffered under Hitler, no one was supposed to mention those whose land was taken for a Jewish homeland in

Palestine. When I came back from my first visit to Jerusalem, I told longtime friend Horace Busby that Palestinians were under siege.

"Don't touch that subject!" he warned.

But in a democracy, are we not beholden to "touch" all subjects that involve our government, our domestic and foreign affairs? Are we not urged as loyal Americans to open all issues up for air?

Once when I lived awhile with an Israeli couple, Aviva and her husband Reuven, we went on a picnic and over-looked the land of the Palestinians. "If they don't have their country," said Aviva, the Jew, "we won't have our country."

PART

NINE

21: What Causes One to Forget a Thousand — And Remember One?

"Thanks be to God, the world is wide,
And I am going far from home!
And I forgot in Camelot
The man I loved in Rome."
—Edna St. Vincent Millay

A writer is concerned with time and memory, wondering what encounter with another was gossamer, what remains. Who was the person who became important and why so? Was the relationship one of friendship? Love? Sex? The writer Gore Vidal said he experienced one thousand sexual encounters by the age of twenty-five. He also indicated he had known true love with only one. Why would this be so? What makes one encounter forever fresh in memory and others like negatives exposed to the sun, the subjects no longer visible?

In my relationship with women, my friendship with Jo has been the longest and most significant. Petite, blond, of Dutch parents, she started work at age fifteen in her hometown of Dayton, Ohio. Like me, she worked afternoons while attending morning high-school classes. By eighteen she was secretary to a colonel in the Pentagon. She was nineteen when she moved to New York and we became roommates. From New York, she moved to Los Angeles, where she worked as a travel agent and later bought FitzPatrick Travel from the well-known maker of travel documentaries, James A. FitzPatrick. Highly successful in her work, she bought a home in Bel Aire, near the Ronald Reagans. She and I, for most of our lives geographically separated, went through marriages and social and economic changes but we always managed to meet at least once a year, in Paris, Tokyo, Hong Kong, Lima, Mexico City or at her place or mine. Her friendship has been a ballast to me. Since we have been supportive of one another, knowing her has been like being on a ship sailing smooth seas. On the other hand, my relationships with men often provided pain and shocks of recognition. They thus became learning experiences. From my years with Andy, I learned that what I thought I would surely remember, I do not. I presumed I would always keep in my mind the moments of our sexual togetherness. What about those thousand or so nights we put our bodies down beside one another and those moments I presumed, at the time, were made in Heaven? Why did they all evaporate? And what remains?

Once I suffered fourth-degree burns. A doctor came to our house and instructed Andy how to apply a medication. Andy then gingerly, tenderly touched my skin and in those moments I felt intimate with him. Perhaps intimacy comes when one feels most vulnerable. It comes as an unexpected gift. It is like a poem. You undergo an experience and later there is the poem of the intimacy, fully revealed. When the Mexican smuggler and I were fleeing from police across a crime-infested area from Tijuana into San Diego neither of us had our minds on sex and yet when we lay hidden from police, each of us afraid and vulnerable, I felt intimate with him. In 1995 I went alone to Mayo Clinic in Rochester, Minnesota, and early one morning I lay on a bed outside an operating room. "Hello," said a voice beside me. It was Dr. Raymond Lee, whom I had met the previous day. Aware of my great love of travel, he talked to me about Italy. "The Renaissance—wasn't that marvelous?" He was more than a surgeon trained to cut and sew. He gave me the wonderful sensation of our embarking—together— on a journey. Casually he said, "Are you ready? I will roll you in." In that moment I felt intimate with him.

In Seoul, I learned how I as a woman tried to ride a vehicle called love to give my life meaning. As to why I devised this scenario, I credit the Alabama general who spoke so pejoratively about Koreans, saying they were "hardly off their all-fours." He termed them "gooks" and inferior "because they are members of the colored race." At that time Bill Shinn was no more than a name on a slip of paper given to me by an Associated Press friend in New York. "Call our Korean stringer there," he had suggested. After returning from the 38th Parallel to Seoul, I phoned Shinn and gushed, "You have a marvelous voice." We agreed to see each other at a United Nations gathering. It was a warm October 20, 1955, and speeches were held outdoors. I looked into a cluster of reporters, attempting to find his face. I could not connect the voice that had spoken to me in perfect English with any of the Asian faces. Later Bill found me and introduced himself and still later he came to the Brando Hotel and we sat in the lobby. In my spirit I rushed to him, in a spontaneous, giving way. I did not employ words so much as eyes and gestures. I used these means to convey this message: here in Korea I want my life to have meaning. You are the one who can help me. I want something different from comfort, even if it is discomfort. I want to make a sacrifice, anything that will help me discover what I am to do with my life.

"Let me represent Korea for you," Bill responded. "This poor country can help you."

Korea was devastated. In Seoul there was hardly any

place to go for a talk. One bitter cold night I accompanied Bill to a bar. It was crowded with lonely U.S. servicemen, none permitted to have an American wife there. Few American female civilians worked there, and servicemen were told not to associate with Koreans. When we entered, a hush came over the GIs. Many were seeing an American woman for the first time in months. After Bill and I climbed on bar stools, a sergeant on my right nudged me and in an angry yet proprietary note almost hissed at me, "You, a white woman ... out with this 'gook'!" His anger propelled him to his feet. "It's disgusting!" He drew a knife, threatening Bill. Luckily, we escaped his range.

With Bill, I sat on straw-matted floors and ate kimchi and other Korean food, using silver chopsticks. Through the night I heard voices from the street that came to me through paper-thin walls of a room we shared. The voices were of vendors passing by. Bill, I asked, what is that man saying? "He wants to sharpen knives." Of another, "He has fish for sale."

One night I told Bill that a doctor had told me I was pregnant. "It is easy not to have a child," Bill replied. "You can have an abortion." I was stunned since I had wanted to find my meaning through him. I left Korea and flew to Japan, where another doctor assured me that I was not and had never been pregnant. But why, I asked, had a Korean doctor said that I was? And why had I felt that I was and my body so indicated? "It seems to have been another case of wanting to be," he explained, "and therefore the body presented certain symptoms of its being true."

In time I admitted to Bill that I attempted to use him, that I was traveling about looking for myself and that I was expecting him and his "land of agony," as Bill called war-torn Korea, to supply my purpose. I realized my reasoning in wanting to give myself away was flawed. It was my encounter with the Korean that made me remember what I knew and had temporarily forgot: not all women are meant to be progenitors and my purpose was beyond bringing yet another child into the world.

In Peru, over a three-year span, I knew Ernesto, a Spaniard born in Barcelona who was an editor at Lima's *La Prensa*. Thirty-two, he looked somewhat like a young Errol Flynn with flashing dark eyes and moustache. He was spontaneous, loved to swim, ride horses and travel. He knew much about music and dance, teaching my body how to move to the *criolla* or native music as well as the cha-cha-cha, samba, mambo, merengue and rumba. I learned the typical dances such as *la marinera* with its mixture of Spanish and African beats and the *vals peruano,* the Peruvian waltz, the best known being *"La Flor de la Canela"*—"Flower of the Cinnamon"—composed by a young woman, Chabuca Granda.

Every day I experienced new discoveries and wrote glowing letters to my friend Jo. Years later, when we were visiting, Jo asked, "Wasn't Ernesto the love of your life?" I said no. I had in my letters shared with her the good times but not his possessiveness, his jealousy. After I met Ernesto and had written my mother, she responded, "Latin men often are extremely jealous." I thought, what does she know? She hasn't lived among them. Ernesto was gallant, generous. In the troubadour mode, he came bearing roses and packaged gifts, with written avowals of enduring love.

One evening we went to the Karamanduka, a restaurant where one may enjoy hot, spicy native food washed down by a popular Peruvian drink called a pisco sour. After we were seated, an orchestra began a *vals peruano*. A Peruvian poet whom Ernesto and I both knew approached, asking me to dance. As I rose to accept, I realized Ernesto would be jealous. I watched him as he stormed from the restaurant. After the waltz, I taxied home. I turned the lock on my front door. It was made of heavy plate-glass panels.

Ernesto, close on my heels, pounded on the door. When

I did not respond, he put a fist through the glass, shattering it. Almost simultaneously a Peruvian policeman, walking his beat, appeared. He demanded I open the door. The two men entered.

"Give him a pisco," Ernesto ordered. I poured three drinks and handed Ernesto a towel for his bleeding hand. We stood sipping drinks as if at a cocktail party. Perhaps all too typically, the policeman ignored me. He talked man-to-man with Ernesto, asking what was the matter with me?

Ernesto had intended to impress me with his "love" — he was willing to lose a hand and risk life itself to totally possess me. But being possessed, I would not be free. Soon thereafter, I left Peru. Later I heard that Ernesto, driving at high speed, was in a collision and died instantly.

In Washington, D.C., in the mid-1960s, I met Hobart Taylor, Jr., who had one of the most brilliant minds I had ever encountered. He was an attorney and held a high government position. His father had made a fortune in Texas real estate. The son, tall, distinguished, and forty-five, also was a millionaire with a Watergate penthouse. One might think he had it all. Except that he was black, and though he had a wife she was not white and he wanted one who was. He divorced his wife and moved into a fashionable home on what is called Embassy Row. Over a mantel he hung an original painting of a tall, slender white woman with blond hair. Then he achieved what must have been his ultimate desire. He married a woman with pink skin and blond hair. Almost immediately he died.

Some seventeen years before his 1981 death, *Houston Post* owner Oveta Culp Hobby had asked me to write a story about Taylor. A flattering story appeared with a large photo. He invited me to dinner. I agreed and suggested I'd broil steak. This was 1964, and white racists were still killing blacks who squired white women. "No," he said to my suggestion, "I've made reservations. At the Jockey Club." It was in fashion and expensive. We drove there in his Lincoln and after being seated, I noted a man at an adjoining table seemed to be suffering body spasms. I tried to ignore the shaking and momentarily imagined he might be suffering from malaria. He was an elderly, white-haired man, seated beside a woman whose face seemed never to have entertained a smile. After ordering drinks, Taylor excused himself to use a telephone, and about the same time the dour-faced woman went to the ladies' room. Her companion, seeing me alone, found his voice and snarled at me, "You, a white woman! And out with a nigger!" His body fell into more convulsions that gave an all-too-clear message: I despise you, I loathe you. You have sunk to the deepest level. How could you do this to me!

Going out with a Korean and later with a black man in Washington, D.C., made me want to know more about the deep chasm that exists between American whites and people with more pigmentation.

I heard Taylor's frank confession that he wanted to marry a white woman. He desired her for a simple reason: she was forbidden, therefore desired. When I darkened my skin and passed as a black woman, I quickly perceived that white men saw me desirable not in spite of but because of my blackness. After finishing *Soul Sister* and a book on Charles Evers, the first black mayor of a Mississippi town, I began researching relationships between interracial couples and why sexual myths and fears play a stellar role in the U.S. form of racism. This book, published in 1972, was entitled *Black-White Sex.*

Although I did my research in the 1960s and 1970s, the taboos on interracial dating and marriage within the United States have not changed much over the years. They are still with us more than a quarter of a century later.

22: The "Great Relation"

"Love, not sex, is the 'way out' of feeling."
—May Sarton, writer

*O*ne day, looking not like any Lothario I had ever seen but reluctant and quite miserable, Roscoe put a proposition before me: in brief he was saying how about sex between you and me. If he had thought about it previously, he had never so indicated. He did not begin his suit with any pawing or power play but rather the two of us were sitting at my dining table, like a long-married couple discussing a problem that had never been given the light of day. I recognized a Roscoe I had not previously seen and knew that his feelings were raw. And I also knew I had to use psychological skills, the kind he had used with me, the kind we all use in developing a friendship: jumping quickly into the other's shoes, trying to see a situation from his or her viewpoint. As we talked, I said from all that he had indicated to me, since he had married Dorothy, and that was like eons ago, he had never been untrue to her. And he said that was the case. But he also said that he wanted to be with a white woman. And so on we went.

The "need" of the black man for the white woman was consuming me in my research and writing of my book *Black-White Sex*. And Roscoe was bringing this truth I had discovered too close to home for comfort. His friends had dubbed him "Horse," and he often referred to himself by that name. Once, he related, male friends and relatives asked, "Horse, have you ever been with a white woman?" He said "No," so they arranged for him to be at one of their homes. He was lying on a sofa, awaiting the paid-for prostitute, "and when she walked in," he said, "I chickened out." He had never been with a prostitute, and he could not bear to touch her. Now perhaps, with me, he was attempting to fulfill his life. And why, if I were such a good friend, could I not supply what was missing?

As we talked, my mind flitted back to a scene of Mother standing by my apartment door, ready to leave, to return to Texas. And with us was Roscoe, who called himself "a coal burner," having dark-chocolate skin pigmentation. He was of medium height, perhaps slightly shorter, and sturdily built. He kept his hair cropped close to his head. In his late sixties, he had retired from two regular jobs and was working as a maintenance man in my apartment building. "Now Roscoe," Mother had said, as she was almost out the door, "you take care of Grace, you know she's up here by herself." Later, recalling that scenario, I asked myself if Mother was being patronizing. Perhaps some would see it that way. But Mother was prescient. She must have known I would be in need of him.

The year was 1963. I had returned to the States from Peru and was working for the *Houston Post*, based in Washington. I had taken an apartment in the Calvert House. I had no furniture, only a couple of boxes with my papers and books and one suitcase with a few clothes. Living around the world in many hotels, I was accustomed to ringing a bell, giving my dirty laundry to a maid or a bellman and getting it back freshly laundered. Soon after I met Roscoe, I handed him a bundle of personal items—bras, panties, slips—asking if he knew someone who would wash them. I knew Roscoe would take the clothes and ask his wife or daughter or some member of his family to wash my undergarments, and this is indeed what happened. He returned them, but when next I saw Roscoe, I was upset: "You did not return everything," I said. "Some items are missing."

The next day he tapped on my door. He held green bills in his hand, ready to deal: "Tell me what I owe you." I was taken aback. I apologized. I admitted I had made no list, I did not know what I had given him. Standing before me, he had forced me to see him as a person, one with whom I had to deal on a one-to-one basis. He had turned the other cheek, offering to pay me for what I presumed had been a wrong. Was he playing Uncle Tom, bowing before Ms. Whitey? Certainly one might see it that way. But in my case, he made me feel ashamed. Beyond that, I was alone and vulnerable. I had made only a few friends in Washington and felt isolated in my walled-in little box, as I called my apartment.

Then came Easter Sunday. I was alone and heard a tap. Opening the door, I saw Roscoe holding a rather absurd, cheap, made-of-synthetics Easter gift. Thrusting the gift—it was not a bunny, but a little white fluffy dog, with large appealing plastic eyes—into my hands, he was gone. Holding the gift, I felt as if my heart had been punctured, and I burst into tears. He had so quickly penetrated my veneer. How had he known me, which largely consisted of layers of loneliness. Having pride, I had wanted to keep that to myself. Now I knew he knew.

Roscoe and I began, slowly at first, to spend an enormous amount of time together. In the years of our relationship, spanning a quarter of a century, we generally saw each other five or six days a week, starting when he would give a tap on my door about seven in the morning, and I would invite him for coffee. After I started to work at the White House and drove a white Buick convertible, I gave Roscoe a set of keys to this car. He had a car, but in case he needed mine, he had use of it. I also gave him keys to

my apartment. Since I was out during the day, he could go
to my apartment, enjoy a hot meal, which was usually
something we had cooked together, listen to music, relax
awhile. For me, it was like a "marriage of convenience."

He provided help especially when I began to take the
pills to darken my skin. I recorded in *Soul Sister* our driving to a beach near Ocean City. He sat under an umbrella
while I was "at work" on my project to darken my skin.
Going and coming, he commented on the corn in the
fields we passed and talked about growing up on a North
Carolina farm. He was one of eleven boys and girls born
to Finnetta and Joseph Dixon. On that trip, Roscoe told
me that since the family was "dirt poor," he had left home
as a teenager and come to Washington. I visualized him, a
raw youth, walking the streets, searching for work, being
repeatedly told, "No, we don't hire colored people."
Eventually he got a job washing pots. "Can you imagine
restaurants having so many pots a man stays busy ten hours
a day washing them!" For awhile he was a cook at
O'Donnell's seafood restaurant, then for many years at
Howard University. Additionally, to gain money, he
repaired radios and televisions. After I returned from my
stay in Mississippi, passing as a black woman, I was emo-
tionally and physically drained. Soon thereafter I went to
doctors who found me in such a weakened condition they
gave me blood, which turned out to be bad blood, traced
to a dope addict. From this 1969 transfusion I developed
a severe bout of serum hepatitis and was near death for
three months. Later, when I was better, sitting at the dining table, talking with Roscoe, I felt dizzy and fainted,
slumping to the floor. Roscoe carried me to my bed. He
said I needed quiet and rest, and he left. But he checked
on me each day.

Often, he talked to me of his life. Rather than being bitter about early hardships, Roscoe had survived on a sense
of humor. In his twenties, he married a young, thin

woman in frail health, who had hoped to study law but who died soon after they were married. Her mother insisted that she be buried with her diamond wedding ring. At the burial, Roscoe told me, "I cried."

"Because she died?" I asked.

"No, because I hated to see that ring disappear. I didn't have it paid for." Then he laughed heartily. He always laughed at the absurd, and that, after all, is most of life.

In 1932 he had married Dorothy, a sturdily built attractive woman with cinnamon-colored skin, of whom Roscoe was most proud. I can never forget his initial description of Dorothy. He said, simply, she was "a good woman." Soon after Roscoe and I became friends, he brought her to my apartment for tea. By bringing Dorothy to my apartment and later by inviting me to his home when several family members were there, Roscoe allowed Dorothy to know me as a friend and not be jealous or resentful of me. That took wisdom on his part. And to a greater extent, on her part.

Roscoe grew a vegetable garden and regularly brought me green beans, potatoes, okra, tomatoes, and often flowers. Learning Roscoe had never flown and never been to New York, I gave him a round-trip airline ticket to New York and arranged his hotel accommodation. But I noticed that when I gave Roscoe a gift or when I did any small favor for him, he was not as pleased as when he gave me a gift or was able to do favors for me.

"Life comes along with special gifts, at various stages," Roscoe told me. "My first big event was our having children. And then the grandchildren came along." He paused: "And then you came along." He always made me feel good, as a person, as a friend. He and I went on my shopping expeditions together, and invariably he arranged his schedule to drive me to the airport when I traveled by plane. Always we were talking, he sharing incidents that happened at home. With their own children grown and away from home, he and Dorothy had taken two boys to raise from the D.C. Welfare Department. Once Roscoe had the boys, Stanley, nine, and Bruce, seven, in his car and was driving in a part of town where the boys' real mama had lived. He didn't think they were aware of the neighborhood, but Bruce piped up, "There's where the woman lives who sells pussy. Sells it for a dollar!"

"I did not know," Roscoe commented to me, "with Bruce's emphasis on a dollar, whether he thought it was not enough or perhaps a great deal of money."

Roscoe drove them to see the ocean. He taught them about the earth, about planting vegetables and flowers. "They had never had their feet on real dirt, the kind of land I knew as a boy." Sitting with me, telling the story, Roscoe added, "I like these boys. I like them just like I did my own boys."

Thus for almost a decade Roscoe and I had enjoyed a friendship, with my thinking of him in the beginning of the relationship in a quite stereotypical way and perhaps his thinking of me in that way also. He did all manner of chores for me—washing my clothes, cleaning my apartment, washing my windows, helping me with the shopping, cooking, planning meals. I did not see him as sexually attractive, and this did not have to do with any moral or societal compunctions, as I was sexually attracted to other black men. At the same time, there was the man-woman aspect: I enjoyed being with Roscoe because he was a man. It would have been a different relationship had he been a woman. Still, I never harbored a thought such as, hey, wonder what he'd be like in bed?

Had Roscoe, in the first stage of our relationship, seen me in a sexual way? I do not know, but since he and I met back in the early sixties, he probably ruled it out. It was soon after the lynchings, and the Klan had hardly stopped shooting blacks for even looking at a white woman. I was the first white woman he had known socially, the first one with whom he drank coffee every morning, ate meals, went on picnics and with whom he'd talk for hours at a time. If that was important for him, it was equally important for me. He was the first black I truly came to know, who shared the intimate details of how it was growing up in white America. To him, more than anyone, I owe the debt for inspiring the early books I wrote on race relations.

For many years I used Roscoe as counselor and psychiatrist. I complained to him about my friend Peter: "He never brings me anything! He comes here, eats my food, drinks my Scotch! And I never get to see him on Saturdays or Sundays!" Roscoe would smile and remind me: "A half loaf is better than no loaf." I always thought he had only Peter and me in mind, but he must have known it was applicable for himself, as well.

Like Topsy, our relationship simply grew, and we never discussed it. Not until the second phase of our relationship, which was only a brief period and resulted from my endless talks with Roscoe, based on my research for *Black-White Sex*. Also, for several years, Roscoe knew there were men in my life, with whom I enjoyed intimate relationships, and he knew the various men, whom he had dubbed "the team." Instead of "How is Peter?" "Paul?" "Cyral?" it was, "How's the team?" With my new research on black-white sex, I began adding new team members, including a black serviceman who had returned from Europe. About this time Roscoe undoubtedly began to think: Hey, dummy, if him, why not me? And it was then that he came to me, looking miserable and suggesting that his own life would not be complete unless he had sex with a white woman.

What I said to him went like this: "You and I have begun a different pattern. We have gone beyond that. You have much that I do not have—family, children, loyal mate. And I have some aspects of life that you do not have. And neither of us will ever have it all." Actually, in retrospect, I believe Roscoe would have been devastated if I accepted his proposition. Just as I had ruled out sex with him, so I believe years earlier he had with me. He knew how to "use" me, however. His bringing up the subject of sex required me to remind him how unique and special our relationship was. I think each of us knew this, but perhaps I had never said it.

Then came our third phase. One day Roscoe retired from his Calvert maintenance work, but he would return to the building to fill in for others, and he did so in order to take me shopping and help me with various chores. It was July 1, 1981, when I awakened at five. I was in my small kitchen facing the front door of my apartment, heating water for tea, when I saw a green slip of paper come sliding under my door. "I'm on the switchboard," the note said. "See you at eight o'clock." I opened the door and waved to Roscoe. I was certain he had consented to work the graveyard shift in order to take me grocery shopping.

That night it turned windy and temperatures plummeted, a strange development for summer. Rainstorms with hail were predicted. I went downstairs, taking Roscoe a small electric stove to keep him warm for the next three hours. Then I made him a thermal jug of hot, sweetened tea. Back in my apartment, I stood in the living room by big windows and looked at the trees dancing in the winds. In those moments I knew how much he meant in my life. Roscoe, more than any other person, helped me survive the research and writing of my experiences living as a black. And later, my experiences living as an American Indian, then as a Mexican wetback. Once, for *The Illegals,* since I planned to cross the border in the trunk of a car, I asked Roscoe to let me practice, to know how it felt to be crouched, hidden in a small, locked space. I climbed into the trunk of his car, he closed the trunk door and drove around town. When we got back to the Calvert garage and

I crawled out of the trunk, he was more nervous than I had ever seen him. "If a policeman had stopped me and inspected that trunk," he said, "there's no way he would have believed my story."

And Roscoe saw me through the writing of the book on the oldest living people in the Americas, *Los Viejos,* and he was with me in spirit as I researched and wrote about problems in the Holy Land. While doing this research, I said to Roscoe that since Bethlehem was in the Orient, "Jesus would not have been white. He would have been a colored man." With his open mind and open heart, Roscoe replied, "What difference does it make?"

Often I would be gone from my apartment for months. Roscoe would later say, "I telephoned. Just to listen to the ring in your apartment."

Once I debated whether to visit Mother or send her five hundred dollars. "Go," Roscoe advised. "Don't forget your most valuable gift to a person is your time." Only now do I realize that none of "the team" got from me what Roscoe did. Nothing important is done without time —and Roscoe had more of my time than any, even "the team." One summer when the number one member of my team was overseas and Roscoe was on vacation, I was aware of missing both—but it was Roscoe who had taken up the larger portion of my heart.

On a summer day in 1982, I attended the fiftieth wedding anniversary of Roscoe and Dorothy at the First Baptist Church near the home where they had lived for half a century. They recited their wedding vows, Roscoe dressed in a new suit, Dorothy in a white gown. All their children, grandchildren and great-grandchildren were there, as well as hundreds of friends and relatives. I was accepted by all, part of the family.

Then one day he suffered a heart attack—he who had never been ill—and almost died.

He still managed to get to the Calvert House, although

he could no longer drive and getting over for a visit took every ounce of his strength. He knew I was going through the most difficult period of my life: my mother, who had fallen and broken a hip, had been placed in a nursing home. I agonized over the situation. Although he could barely walk, Roscoe called a taxi and came to counsel me.

Using a cane, he got himself to a chair. I sat at his feet, crying. Nothing had ever been so difficult for me—not any of my experiences living as a black, or Indian or wet-back—as not being able to help my mother. Roscoe sat talking with me, reminding me that I had an older sister. But, I told him, I felt I should give up my apartment and take care of Mother.

"Is that what your mama would want?"

"No," I said.

Roscoe helped me understand that I had to accept what I could not change.

On a hot August day in 1985, I took a metro and rode past the big D.C. stadium and on to Minnesota Avenue, a stop where I left the metro. I saw a taxi and hailed it and got to 4503 Jay Street, and although I had said I would arrive for a visit "around three," I was arriving early, around two-thirty.

Roscoe, looking smaller, thinner than I had ever seen him, was on the front porch, sitting, waiting. I had been to this home several times and enjoyed Dorothy's good meals. I knew that Roscoe had paid six thousand dollars for it when he married Dorothy, and that in 1985 it was valued at a hundred thousand. I recalled Roscoe's telling me how proud he was to have the home debt-free. A sprinkler was dousing life-giving water on a magnolia tree and flowers, and suddenly as I entered into Roscoe's world I was aware of a cooler, fresher air than flows in my neighborhood of tall buildings and concrete and smoke-clogged streets.

I stepped onto the porch and embraced my dear friend,

whose body now seemed more bones than human flesh. He had told me on the phone that he had lost his appetite. He and I walked inside and began talking, and Dorothy did not appear for quite awhile, although we both knew she was an earshot away. Later, she joined us.

On another visit to Roscoe and Dorothy, he was able to sit in the living room for only a short period. Since his illness, he had been in and out of hospitals, and he had now exacted from Dorothy a promise: he would never again enter a hospital. He was choosing his way of dying, and his way was to be at home and never take another morsel of food. He merely stopped eating. Dorothy respected his wishes. After awhile he retired to his bed, and I accompanied him, sitting on the bed beside him, holding onto one of his hands, neither of us talking.

I then walked into the living room, and their elder daughter, also named Dorothy, came in. She had not liked me in the beginning, which was only natural—wasn't her father playing Uncle Tom to this whitey? But years had passed and love has a way of widening its circle. Now we fell spontaneously into each other's arms, and her mother, the senior Dorothy, joined us. The three of us stood holding onto one another, crying and feeling the impending loss. Somehow in our union, in that moment at least, the burden of Roscoe's leaving us was slightly less heavy.

Suddenly—and when one loves, a loss always comes "suddenly"—he was gone.

The novelist Henry James recognized that what he called "the great relation" between men and women is carried on most interestingly, perhaps even most passionately, when the parties involved cannot or dare not take each other to bed. In our present preoccupation with the purely sexual we have lost sight of this truth. Over and over again, in modern books, writers bring their characters to orgasm, forgetting that the news of orgasm has long since reached us. In an essay on Henry James, the writer John Aldridge reminds us that "the inexhaustible mystery, the drama that is forever refreshed because it is nowhere ever the same, is to be found in the nature of the people in the relationship being consummated."

PART

Coming of Age

TEN

23: Ecuador —
Living with los Viejos

"Our life is what our thoughts make of it."
—*Marcus Aurelius*

When we define aging as growing old, what does it mean? When does one get "old"? John Howard Griffin, author of *Black Like Me*, once told me, "Growing old — that's for your parents, other people. It never happens to you." Exceptional age does not automatically invite feebleness or decrepitude. Does anyone grow old without feeling it? I felt as young as I did at twenty or thirty in 1974, when at age fifty-one, I went to stay awhile among the oldest people in the southern hemisphere. They lived in a virtual Shangri-la in southern Ecuador. Did they have secrets for a long and healthy life? Did they have a special diet? Was it exercise? A mental attitude toward others and life in general? Perhaps I could bring back some recipes for healthy living, for stalling that condition we call "old and feeble."

First I flew to the Ecuadorian capital of Quito, then I traveled by bus through the towering Andes. After a bus journey of some five hundred miles, I saw the "Sacred Valley" of Vilcabamba from a distance, as harmoniously arranged as if it had been executed on a canvas and set in a frame.

Once I began living in the village, I felt stress fall from my body as if I had suddenly shed excess weight. As on a long and tranquil ocean voyage, time seemed almost suspended. The stillness suggested that the valley might have been entombed for a millennium. Until the seventies, there was no all-purpose road that led into Vilcabamba. Nestled at an altitude of forty-five hundred feet among mountains covered with lush tropical foliage, the village rested untouched by neon, mercantile business and those smoking portents of a polluted environment. It reminded me at a glance of the mystical celestial city of James Hilton's *Lost Horizon.*

While there, I spent time with *los viejos,* the old ones, some of whom were well over a hundred. One man, Gabriel Sánchez, reportedly was 113. He did not live within the confines of the village, but I borrowed a horse in Vilcabamba and following directions set out to find him. I slowly ascended into the mountains, but soon the Andean terrain became too rugged, and I dismounted, leading the horse, wondering, even if I got to the top, if I would possibly find Gabriel Sánchez there. But eventually I found him, atop a mountain called El Chaupi. When I arrived at the mountaintop, I immediately sat down, exhausted. But Sánchez continued standing, his hands on the top of a hoe. Finally, at my insistence, he sat beside me. Addressing me in Spanish, with a title implying respect, as if I might be a medical doctor or a professor, he asked, "Little doctor, how did you get up here?"

It had not been easy for me, and I wondered how such an old one could have made the climb. As we talked, he was outgoing and candid. Perhaps, because I was a stranger—and one often reveals what is most real to one who is only passing by—he was soon telling me of the saddest aspect of his life, the loss of a son. The river currents caught the boy and he drowned. Sánchez's eyes filled with grief as he relived his story of loss.

About five-foot-five, with an enormous chest from decades of climbing, Sánchez was wearing an old but clean shirt and trousers. Studying him, I saw him as an integral part of the mountain, almost like another rock, as much an ingredient of the soil as its mineral contents. He had lived all of his life close to nature. He had never known an office, never been barricaded behind walled rooms. Each day, Sánchez rose at five and climbed to the top of the mountain to work a field, not for himself but for a rich hacienda owner, his *patrón* or boss. Why, I asked, did he continue to work?

"I would be ashamed, sitting at home, my arms folded, doing nothing," he said. Under the hacienda system, when Sánchez worked a large field for his patrón, he was permitted to cultivate a small plot for himself and his family. Peasants such as Señor Sánchez have never really known a money system, since the master pays not in cash but in seeds, animals and the use of his land. Surviving under such a system would tax the physical strength and toughness of a man a quarter his age, but Sánchez seemed to take it in stride.

He struggled for the barest essentials, such as water. All of his water had to be brought from the Rio San Pedro. From the river Sánchez must trek an arduous hour to his hut. One day I arrived at his hut and watched him as he trudged in from his labors. A distraught Maria Petrona, his ninety-six-year-old wife, told him the harness for the burro had been stolen. Without the harness, the granddaughter Maria could not lead an old blind burro up and down the steep, twisting mountain path to bring water from the river. Their lives depended on the burro and the harness.

Sánchez immediately sought a solution. He gathered bits of discarded leather, only two or three inches in length, that he had saved for just such an emergency, and began the tedious process of nailing the pieces together. I stood watching, and attempted to make conversation, but he did not reply. All of his brain cells were applied to his one art: survival. His long years testified that he was good at that. Necessity demanded that he use his brain or perish.

Eventually, after watching him for a couple of hours at his slow task, I asked: "Señor Sánchez, how much does a harness cost?"

"Oh, little one, fifteen sucres," he replied and made it sound as if it were thousands of dollars. Quickly calculating the sum he needed to be about sixty cents, I handed him some paper bills that amounted to fifteen sucres. He thanked me as though I had paid off the mortgage on a home. Then he lit candles, knelt and prayed to his God for this miracle. Getting up from his knees, he then prepared to walk a distance of some ten miles into the village to buy the harness.

Although I had doled out a few sucres on that occasion, I was not in the remote village to be patronizing but to learn. I needed the villagers to "take me in," to provide a place for me to sleep, to provide me with food to eat, to show me how to live through my last years with dignity, spirit and fortitude. I lived in their dirt-floored primitive huts, and I slept on their beds of rough-hewn wooden boards. I often took my meals with Micaela Quezada, slender and erect in a floor-length black dress with a shawl draped around her head. "I am 104 years old," she told me. Having by choice never married, the old woman proudly added, "I am a virgin," just as another woman might boast of a prized diamond necklace.

I watched this woman in her kitchen. Growing old for Micaela Quezada, despite her dire poverty, was easier than for those aging in the idle clinical "comfort" of nursing homes and sanitoriums with their minds turned inward, often tranquilized out of reality. Señorita Quezada cooked regularly for a nephew, and she remained forever busy with her hands, working in her garden, building fires, preparing food. Her spartan kitchen occupied a small corner of a room with an iron stove and bits of firewood. A small shelf near the stove held only a can for cooking fat and containers of salt and pepper. She kept none of the canned goods and the array of condiments many modern cooks deem indispensable in preparing meals.

Micaela Quezada cooked only the cheapest cuts of meat, such as the heart, brain, tongue, liver, tripe and gizzards, and she did so because these were affordable. Villagers raised each animal themselves and they contained no poisons from large commercial meat-packing plants. The *viejos* ate a natural diet: wild game, wild berries, nuts, whole grains, vegetables and fruits, especially oranges that were plentiful in the valley. Until recent years, the *viejos* never had white sugar.

Visitors to Vilcabamba claim there is "something special" about the valley, and yet the *viejos* resemble millions of dirt-poor country folk everywhere — hard-working, uncomplicated and relatively serene. They live hard, sparse lives, and they have few earthly goods. They are well below the poverty line, yet they seem to have been bred for a special brand of gentility, a freedom from the corrosive effects of hatred, an immunity to violence. With these qualities, they have accumulated huge reserves of goodwill.

I also came to know Manuél Ramón, who told me he was 110. "I have always worked," said Ramón, whose face radiated the force of his character. When I felt his strong biceps and praised his ability to climb mountains I could barely ascend and to work from sunup to sunset in a field of maize, he bowed his head shyly, and confessed in his modest way: "It is no great thing I do." He convinced me that the human body over millions of years has been fashioned to serve Señor Ramón and all the rest of us in strenuous, daily activities. We are designed to live as *los viejos* live, pushing ourselves to a physical limit.

Old age does not necessarily consign one to a limbo of

uselessness. We admire the active, productive life of a Verdi, Voltaire, Hugo, Michelangelo, Picasso, Casals, Toscanini, Cervantes, Goethe, Tennyson, Wells, Shaw, Sophocles, Santayana, Colette and Grandma Moses, to name a few. Some of the greatest musicians, writers, painters, poets reached their peaks well after a so-called retirement age.

While no one has been able to verify their ages exactly, *los viejos* undoubtedly are very old. No one, however, wishes to add years to his or her life, if in doing so one becomes feeble and senile. The "secret" of *los viejos* of the Sacred Valley simply instructs us to exercise more; to eat less, particularly less fatty meat; to lessen the stress in our lives by learning to love ourselves and by becoming lovable to others; to get enough sleep; and finally to keep spirit, laughter and love in our lives. They remind us, by their vigor, that good health depends less on medicines than on a congenial adaptation to environment.

In observing my remarkable father and mother as they aged and also the old ones of Vilcabamba, I saw they had something in common: a philosophy of life that enabled each of them to harbor goodwill toward others, to do good work and leave the rest up to a greater power, in which they fervently held a firm faith. In the case of my father and my mother, as they grew quite old, I saw a greater flexibility in their acceptance of others and the weal and woe of life's circumstances. Like Sánchez, they did what they could to solve a problem, and if it was too great they relegated it to a higher power. In the United States, some studies have indicated that faith in a greater power, regardless of the type of religion to which one adheres, does indeed add years and better health to one's life.

"I never felt old," Mother told me when at age ninety-two she fell and broke a hip. Then for the first time, being so incapacitated, she knew how "old" feels. Like my mother and father, I was blessed with a good, healthy body. In 1994, I was a back-seat passenger in an automobile involved in a bad accident. Nerve endings were severely damaged, I needed stitches in my head and hand and from later complications I underwent surgery. I could barely walk and did so with pain. It was an ironic turn that after traveling the world and tempting the perils in far climes, I was injured only a short distance from my front door. I was seventy-one and again underwent a drastic life change, more so than when I changed from white to black or lived as an Indian or wetback. Being incapacitated reminded me, as no other experience had done, of life's most precious values. "It's terrible what that car accident did to you," commented a woman in my apartment building.

"Today," I responded, "I saw a man with one leg."

"That doesn't help," she said.

I said it did help. Suffering can instruct. He gave me a new sense of living, reminding me—as injuries and illnesses do—that each of us is fragile and all we really possess is the moment we call now.

Epilogue

"If you will, you are free. If you will, you have no one to
complain of, no one to accuse."
— *Epictetus, born 50 B.C., a slave*

For many years, traveling the world, I was looking for ways to develop my vocal cords, to speak, to say who I was, what I was about. Then, coming to realize that I had a voice, I wanted to use it for a purpose, to speak for others as well as myself.

I lived the lives of the Other: a black, an Indian, a wetback. From the beginning I had credentials to "pass" as the Other, having lived a lifetime not as a minority but nevertheless a Second Sex, one Other Than a Man.

In each instance, assuming a mask of the Other, I was astonished that so many in authority saw me as a lesser person, often no more than a cipher. In some instances, living my research, I took risks that put my life in danger. But life is not the supreme value. It is courage. Having a desire to know one's self. Setting about to give a meaning to one's life. These, for me, were the supreme values. I never sought danger for the sheer thrill of it but rather to have a learning experience, to make that experience count toward shaping a life that could "speak" of some purpose.

As a woman, I have the right, no less than a man, to say and to prove that I value the reasons for living above mere life. Throughout history, men have traditionally given life supreme dignity by their dangerous pursuits. In the beginning, man struggled against wild animals, ran grave risks, put his life in jeopardy to elevate the prestige of the horde or the clan. Later, man climbed the highest peaks, sailed the oceans, went to the moon. And in doing so, he did not give life itself priority; rather it was there to be used, to serve ends more important than itself. It is not giving life, but risking life, for some cause beyond the comfort of daily existence, that raises us above the beasts in the field. Perhaps the worst curse put upon woman was the idea that she should think of herself as frail, in need of a protector, put on earth as a progenitor.

We in America, where our diversity has made us strong, are still in a "testing" stage of our great democracy. Democracy assumes that all men and women are created equal, under the law. It assumes that no group, white or black, Christian, Muslim or Jew, should have preferential treatment. We all face a great challenge: to so live our lives that we are worthy of a democracy. We can achieve our great aims only if we truly accept the Other, of whatever sexual orientation, religious creed or degree of skin pigmentation, not as being different, not as inferior, but like ourselves an authentic human being. Like Miguel de Unamuno I like to say, "I am a human being; no other human being do I deem stranger."

Strangers became just like me—when I walked in their shoes.

About the Author

*G*race Halsell is the author of twelve books, including *Soul Sister*, in which she related her experiences living as a black in Mississippi and Harlem; *Bessie Yellowhair*, the story of her life on a Navajo reservation in Arizona and as a Navajo nursemaid in Los Angeles; *The Illegals*, detailing her experience swimming the Rio Grande to enter Texas as a Mexican wetback; and *Journey to Jerusalem*, a description of the life she lived among Christians, Muslims, and Jews in the strife-torn Holy Land.